Commissioned by God

To Andrew & Anne
With all good wishes.

[signature]

P19

Commissioned by God

Hugh Sawers

Matador
9 Priory Business Park
Kibworth Beauchamp
Leicestershire LE8 0RX, UK
Tel: (+44) 116 279 2299
Fax: (+44) 116 279 2277
Email: books@troubador.co.uk
Web: www.troubador.co.uk/matador

ISBN 978 1783065 097

British Library Cataloguing in Publication Data.
A catalogue record for this book is available from the British Library.

Typeset in StempelGaramond Roman by Troubador Publishing Ltd
Printed and bound in the UK by TJ International, Padstow, Cornwall

Matador is an imprint of Troubador Publishing Ltd

*A word of appreciation is due to my daughter
Gillian Gray for all her unstinting help and
assistance in the compilation of this work.
Well done Gill.*

*Cover illustration depics the 'Greek' Thomson Church
of Scotland building, located at Caledonia Road,
Glasgow, which was first attended by the Sawers family
in the early nineteen forties.*

*With thanks to Sam Gray for cover photography
and to Jim Brown for author photography.*

*To Rena my lifelong partner and loving companion
without whose influence I would have been
so much poorer*

Chapter One

In a mood of heightened excitement and enthusiasm I presented myself for matriculation at Glasgow University at the beginning of October 1963. All the obstacles in the way of continuing formal education that had so engaged me throughout my childhood and youth had been overturned. The prospect of academic rigour during the five years of study ahead was truly welcome. Massive gaps in reading in particular would require to be addressed. Above all, I was most vulnerable in terms of my knowledge of the faith and of the attendant structures of the Church within which I now hoped to serve. Could there be, I asked myself, a more challenging or thrilling prospect?

We gathered that first morning at Trinity College and I came face to face with the men who had also emerged from the selection process and who would be my companions and, in some cases, my particular friends over the next five years. In this first encounter I have to say that my first impressions were not as positive as I had anticipated. I had, in a strange way, expected almost to be overwhelmed by their collective aura of sanctity and holiness. I had no such pretensions, but I rather hoped that my fellow students' manifest uprightness and glowing Christian conviction would reach out and begin an immediate process of transformation within myself. No such communication or intimation was felt. In truth they looked a very ordinary gathering of disparate men. Any need for immediate dramatic change in my personal spiritual growth was not hastened by my first encounters. This process, it seemed, would have to wait. What was more immediate was the laying before us of a schedule of study.

Our first two years were designated Pre-Divinity. We were to study four subjects from the ordinary MA curriculum over two years. There was a little latitude for choice here. I elected to take English language and literature and British history in year one. I proposed to study moral philosophy and European history in year two. These subjects were to be taken at Gilmorehill, together with all the other Arts Faculty students who were embarking on their MA degree course. Meanwhile we would attend classes at Trinity College in New Testament Greek. Before commencing our divinity studies proper in year three, we would be required to pass the necessary entrance examination in New Testament Greek. Coincidental with this study at Trinity College we would also prepare for the necessary Bible examination ahead of acceptance to our course in theology. If we desired to obtain qualification as Licentiate in Theology, on the completion of our five years' work, then independently of all our prescribed course work, we should also require further passes in two more subjects at the higher level in the Scottish Education Department 'Highers' or from the university prelims. I elected to study Higher history and Higher mathematics. Taken together, the work involved during the two years of Pre-Divinity was very onerous indeed.

With our workload determined, the classes followed very swiftly. Our English lectures were located in the central and oldest building complex within the university. There was, therefore, no absence of atmosphere as we made our way under venerable arches within the cloister area. The well-tended quadrangle lawns loaned a pleasing aspect to the setting for our intended learning. I proceeded along my way, entranced by a present sense of hi   st. The lecture room was as antique as its outsi   setting. The students were gathered in steeply rising curved tiers, amphitheatre fashion, focussed towards the podium and the lecturer. The lectures were, sadly I thought, rather prosaic, and the lecturer remote and seemingly indifferent, giving the appearance of someone who found his work rather tedious. Our main preoccupation, even so, was to attempt to become adept at the all-important task of note-taking. All my life I had encountered difficulties as a left-hander. Here was yet more evidence. Every seat had an accommodating arm to the side to facilitate note-taking. It was at the wrong side for left-handers. To overcome the difficulty I had to stretch across my body from left to right to find the fixed surface upon which to write.

Within a fortnight or so we were required to submit our

first essay. This was calculated, no doubt, to provide the faculty with the first evidence, or otherwise, of our basic background and language ability. We were invited, in essay form, to outline and catalogue the literature that had influenced us from earliest childhood. I was honest in my essay, explaining that resorting to newspapers had been greatly influential in my formative years. My lecturer was singularly unimpressed and made it most clear that newsprint, by no stretch of the imagination, could be categorised as literature. In assessing my essay as beta gamma, I obtained from him the poorest mark that I was ever to receive in the course of the next five years. This experience, and similar early ones, determined me to focus on the hopes and, it may be, the prejudices of the lecturer, and regurgitate answers more to his liking. This approach, I quickly found, enabled good to better than good results to follow in disciplines like English literature and moral philosophy where there resided a large degree of subjectivity.

Outside the lecture room began the interplay of human relationships and friendships which university life so readily offers. The amorphous gathering of the early days settled and little knots of like-minded men emerged and fell into conversation. In a short space, the germs of friendships developed as I met up with Jim Guthrie and Bryan Tomlinson, two who were already friends from past common Church connections, but there was room for three and so we walked together from Gilmorehill to Lyndoch Terrace and Trinity College, talking together as we made our way to lunch. Lunch at Trinity was a communal affair, where the food was monitored and served by fellow students in rotation. The teaching staff shared lunch together with their students and an air of friendly informality pervaded the whole scene, conducive to advancing warmth and friendship. I discovered along this route that Jim Guthrie came from Knightswood and that by background he had been a time-served engineer in the shipbuilding industry. He was about four years younger than me and since I had just turned twenty-eight, it remained a mystery to me that he should be joining our mature student intake which had a minimum starting age of twenty-five. However, since I had appeared in an almost miraculous fashion at Trinity, there could be little quibble with a man defying the regulations by a mere one year. Jim, by virtue of his working background, could be said to have his feet firmly on the ground and it could not be said of him that 'he was so heavenly minded as to be of no earthly use!' The same assessment could be made with regard to Bryan Tomlinson. My early estimate concerning him, and I have had no reason since to have changed it, was that Bryan's Christianity was of the robust practical sort. 'Fools were not to be suffered gladly' would be axiomatic for Bryan. We had been thrown together and we were happy in each other's company. I am aware that I have already indicated that spiritual growth was, in my case, something devoutly to be sought. Jim and Bryan were not conspicuous candidates to assist my further development in this quarter but help was at hand. By a strange quirk, the Free Church of Scotland had deigned to allow one of its students to commence his studies within the environment of the Church of Scotland at our Pre-Divinity stage. The student was Ken Smith and I almost immediately sensed that he was in danger of being isolated. I introduced myself, and Ken was drawn into our intimate group. He was a singularly upright man with a characteristically serious Free Church demeanour. Beyond this outward appearance, it was possible to occasionally trigger a sense of fun from within him. He was a truly good companion and the three others of our group came to admire him in so many ways. Ken was undoubtedly holy. If, for example, we happened into a tearoom or the university refectory, Ken, before touching his scone or whatever, would close his eyes, bow his head and offer thanks – and Ken's thanks were never short. We came to accept his piety but I was never tempted to emulate it in these terms. I was rapidly coming to see the wide gaps in the theological stance of different groups of my fellow students. There were those whom I quickly identified as conservative evangelical Christians. If there were holy and pious fellow students to be found, and there were, then this group provided them. They either were, or tended towards, Christian fundamentalism in their expression of their faith. This issued directly from their view of scripture, which was that it was inerrant and not, therefore, open to critical questioning. Metaphorically, I shrank from all such views, and holiness, if it came dressed in this garment, was a less attractive proposition. At the other end of the spectrum were to be found the out-and-out liberals, whose views outstripped transcendency itself.

Any thing and every event could be intellectually rationalised. One need not be detained by the innumerable contradictions within scripture. An explanation in human terms would be readily to hand. From within this group, generally speaking, emerged those who could be designated as career ministers; almost invariably men who were academically able, but rarely ever in a position to attest their faith as flowing from a definitive experience of conversion. Somewhere, lodged between these polarised extremes were, naturally enough, the moderates. Men who viewed the dogmatism of the fundamentalist and the airy-fairyness of the liberal as an uncongenial resting place and alien to their sense of how God, in Christ, was to be represented. God was in Christ and that of itself presented a mind-blowing mystery that overturned the constricting boundaries of fundamentalism and equally demanded a rigour of sensitivity and spiritual awareness frequently absent among liberals. In summary: the fundamentalists were too holy and the liberals insufficiently so. Polarising along this route had taken place in a twinkling and the student body settled down to meet the challenge of forthcoming ministry according to their own lights.

Outwith university, life progressed apace. Dr Steven, my minister at Queen's Park West Church and my mentor, took a benign and scholarly interest in my progress and insisted in offering some help with what, to me, were the vagaries of Greek. I had discovered that, with no foreign language background at all, Greek presented quite a challenge, and Dr Steven endeavoured to lay low some of the obstacles in my way with regard to the complexities of Greek grammar. I think he found me, in this department, less talented than he would have expected but he was much too kind to say so.

New experiences awaited me on, as it were, the domestic or local church level. As soon as I had met the requirements of the Church Selection Board, my minister reckoned that I would greatly benefit from being ordained as a church elder. Accordingly, I was rapidly ordained and found myself within the company of the ruling elders of my congregation. I grasped immediately Dr Steven's impact upon the spiritual guidance of the congregation through the Kirk Session. He possessed a serene competence born of long experience of the matters under review. He dealt with conflicting views in a most even-handed and diplomatic fashion. Potential dissent was sensitively deflected and harmony and cohesion maintained. As a moderator he had clearly won the confidence and admiration of his fellow elders. I could not but benefit from his exemplary conducting of the Kirk Session. I was immediately allocated a district to oversee at a pastoral level. This mainly entailed visiting the homes within the district in advance of the coming Communion season. In the course of the visit, the members' communion cards were delivered and the visit intended as a means of strengthening fellowship and developing the elder's awareness and needs of the individual members within his care. It was clear that the elder's visit, properly conducted, was a vital tool in maintaining and enhancing the appeal of the congregation to the member. In circumstances where the member was indifferent to, or cold towards, the church, then here was the real platform from which to attempt to influence views and encourage warmth in the direction of fuller involvement and support. All this is easier to state than to implement, as I was to find. A fair number of visits were necessary to sufficiently secure the confidence and goodwill of errant members, but I relished the challenge. My experience gained during this spell as an elder was, as Dr Steven had well understood, a time of empowerment. I had barely dipped my toe into the vast sea of challenges as far as preparation for my future life's work was concerned, but a start had been made.

Progress was instantly necessary relative to Church worship and my place within it. Obviously I had no previous experience in this area and in this respect I was again in a totally distinct position. Without exception, divinity students at my stage were already acquainted with reading at church services. They would have had experience in leading prayer and almost certainly they would have preached. I was completely without experience in all these departments.

Dr Steven, who had a keen sense of the fittingness of all things, explained that, over thirty years previously, his first act of public ministry had involved him reading from the psalms. He had been be-gowned in the preaching robe of one of his Aberdeen University divinity professors who subsequently passed on the gown to him as a gift. At our 6.30 p.m. service, late in 1963, Dr Steven slipped that same gown around my shoulders, offered prayer, and we were both conducted into the sanctuary where, in the course of the service, I read from psalm 27, as had my minister so many years before, these stirring and memorable words:

> 'The Lord is my light and my salvation; whom shall I fear?
> The Lord is the strength of my life; of whom shall I be afraid?'

I cannot estimate the impact of those words upon the congregation, but most assuredly, I was deeply and lastingly moved. As in this small way I was ministering, so I was being ministered to! I continued to assist Dr Steven throughout the early months of 1964 by reading scripture regularly at the morning and evening services and thus gradually gained confidence in the face of large, but always sympathetic, congregations.

The academic year sped past and I obtained good results in both English language and literature and British history at Gilmorehill. I had also applied myself to the task of converting Ordinary passes to Higher passes in history and mathematics at the summer diet of Scottish Education Department examinations. I was successful in obtaining Higher history and fell just short of success in mathematics, being awarded a compensatory Ordinary pass in the latter. This was of no value since I already possessed one. The difficulty with Higher maths was that I was endeavouring to self-tutor and I should have recognised that, even with an aptitude for the subject, proper professional guidance was a necessity. Steady, if unspectacular, progress had been made with New Testament Greek and the entrance examination was on track for the next year. All in all, I had enjoyed the new disciplines and felt that I had done justice to them.

Over the summer, the darkest of shadows descended upon our congregation. Dr Steven, hitherto a robust man of fifty-six years, quite suddenly became less so. The congregation was not privy to the nature or the extent of his weakness. One happy feature of the year was that Dr and Mrs Steven had been able to undertake a rare holiday abroad together to the Holy Land. In a note, dated May 12th, that my minister penned from Jerusalem, he expressed his great pleasure, in prospect, of leading prayers at St Andrew's Church of Scotland there.

Dr Steven weakened throughout the summer and was unable to conduct public worship. He wrote briefly to me on August 5th from Ballater, indicating that he had required a further four pints of blood at hospital in Aberdeen, but now felt the benefit. He went on to say that chronic anaemia was proving a stubborn business and the likelihood was that he would not be allowed back to work for a time. I received his letter and realised the extent of his illness if not its name. My dear friend and mentor was dead within weeks. I experienced a mingling of deep personal grief, together with a sense of profound gratitude for all the gifts of grace and transparent goodness that God had so richly laid upon him. A good man had gone from the Church.

This sad and unexpected event within our congregation gave rise to the need to secure a successor to our late minister. A Vacancy Committee was duly formed and given the task of securing a worthy replacement. It had to be the measure of my new-found higher profile within our fellowship that I, together with sixteen other members, was nominated to the Vacancy Committee. The search was quickly begun and from the outset I began to discover something of the mysterious nature of our Vacancy Committees. Our elected secretary was Miss Jean McFarlane, to whom all recommendations and applications were made in the first instance. Our committee, very properly, considered these in full session. Insights and critical comments were called for. Second opinions were sought, largely from senior-positioned clergy in the parish or university. It became clear to me that there were particular spheres of influence around. If a candidate's perceived theological position was not in accord with the mind of the senior coterie within our committee, that would be the end of that candidate's hopes. Where there were grey areas, there was further intrigue. Miss McFarlane had worked previously as secretary for the redoubtable Andrew Herron, Clerk to the Presbytery of Glasgow, and he was not slow to offer his own judgement and insights as to the merits, or otherwise, of particular candidates. This system, in reality, did not seemingly leave a great deal to the influence of the Holy Spirit, who, after all, was meant to lead us into all truth. I was being given into a situation wherein I detected the merest hint of scepticism stirring within as I sought to collaborate in the high and holy task of finding our next minister. Soon we were settled into groups of four and sent out on our commission. We travelled mainly round central Scotland and where a positive response was given, another group would visit in order to substantiate the interest. In this manner we narrowed down the list of candidates to a shortlist. Three candidates emerged with solid support.

The first candidate, from the Borders, upon examination, to my mind represented ministry from the extreme wing of the conservative evangelical part of the Church and to his credit he did not attempt to hide these credentials. His type of ministry, by general consent, would sit most oddly against that of our former minister. He descended to a firm third place but he was not without a measure of support in the committee. The two other candidates vied for first place. My impression of the first of the remaining two was that he would never bear comparison with Dr Steven in any intellectual or scholarly count. He had been aware of our intended presence and I gained the impression that his true theological stance had not necessarily been displayed and that his service on the morning of our main visit had been somewhat tailored.

Some of us represented that view at our afternoon meeting that same day. In consequence of our reservations, half the committee returned to his evening service and, apart from the absence of a meaningful congregation, the service, in my estimate, was in no way uplifting and was characterised by a quite different theological stance from the morning service. In the event, my later expressed doubts were not widely shared and he remained strongly in contention.

The second of the two remaining candidates, from the east of Scotland, impressed me as, by a distance, the most likely of all in contention. He had a crisp and assured manner and conducted, in my view, a thoughtful and meaningful act of worship. Realising that Dr Steven would be regarded by the congregation as virtually irreplaceable, here was a man, I thought, who would not suffer comparison as a pale imitation. He appeared to have strengths and, I hoped, virtues that would be different. My only caution was that instead of my late minister's gentleness, this chap might offer a touch of brusqueness. We had taken a considerable time to narrow down our field of candidates, and short of the three men heading our list we could see no other likely possibilities from amongst the many others that we had considered. Before moving to a final vote that we sensed would be contentious, it was finally agreed, at my prompting, that the committee would transfer their trust to the remaining candidate if the first choice decided against acceptance of our invitation. The man from the east emerged as our choice for sole nominee by nine votes to eight and he was duly invited. After some thought, he declined. He had determined that he still had challenges before him in his present charge. Accordingly, the remaining candidate was approached and was pleased to accept our invitation.

Our new minister's first service in our midst was conducted at our neighbouring church, Camphill Queen's Park, with which we united during the holiday months of July and August. My sense of misgiving was acutely quickened as I listened to him. We were hearing a man of firm and steely conviction coming from the evangelical wing of the Church. This was not the man, I judged, we had thought, as a committee, we had chosen. I was experiencing a steep learning curve in terms of Christian transparency, or the lack of it. Would this, I wondered, be rife within the Church, where ministers could be seen to present an attractive image in order to pursue their calling? Could such men have persuaded themselves that, for Christ's sake, the ends justified the means?

My alarm had less to do with me and much to do with the future health of the congregation. Would our new minister carry forward the good spirit and loyal and generous support that previous ministers had engendered in this place over past decades or would a sense of disappointment and disillusion come to pervade its witness?

Within a week or so of settling down, the new minister paid a visit to our home. He acknowledged my past association with Dr Steven and said that he very much hoped that I would assist him in a similar way. I indicated that his invitation was kind and that I would be pleased to assist in any way that he considered appropriate. He invited me to read for him the following Sunday morning and, before leaving, he offered appropriate prayer, looking forward to our further happy association. I read for him as arranged and I was never again invited to share any service with him.

I had been most anxious not to, in any way, hint at my initial and growing reservations throughout my very brief encounters with our minister. He had either received intelligence concerning me, or had simply concluded that his undertakings given so freely could justifiably be overturned. I did not have to wait long before discovering something more of the personality and character of our new man. At the first Kirk Session convened by our new moderator, I was instantly struck by the singular lack of warmth in the remarks he made concerning his predecessor. They clearly had been poles apart theologically and his comments cemented this opinion. Far more importantly, he intervened in a debate that had arisen on the issue of a Total Abstainers Movement that had been attempting to gain recognition by the National Church. The keen elder who was proposing that our congregation should associate with this movement indicated that the recent General Assembly had approved of their agenda for the Church. The moderator confirmed this to be so and urged the Kirk Session to sign up for membership. I could not believe what I was hearing. I had attended my first General Assembly in May and had followed the debates very keenly. Strangely enough, who should I also have spotted in the other visitors' gallery but our prospective minister. He and I were both present at the very debate that was now being discussed. The subject under debate was whether or not the General Assembly would embrace the Total Abstainers Movement within the Church as the approved position of the Church on the use of alcohol. The Assembly declined to be identified with the movement in this manner but accepted that it represented a point of view.

Either our new minister was asleep throughout that debate or he was giving vent to his own views on the matter. He was certainly not representing the view of the General Assembly accurately to his Kirk Session. I was appalled and saddened but said nothing. We were now being led by a man, I suspected, with narrow evangelical views allied with obvious piety. He presented to me the image of the sort of minister that I could never admire or respect, but meantime the present situation had to be endured.

I was soon back at university, and lectures in moral philosophy and European history were the order of the day and both held my attention. Class examinations came and went without difficulty. My keenness for history in general was measured by my obtaining second place amongst divinity students in the final European history examination of my second year.

In the course of the year, having systematically read the entire Bible from cover to cover, I also stretched well beyond the seventy per cent pass mark and was thus able to overcome a very necessary hurdle. The subtleties of Greek grammar were sufficiently dealt with as to permit me to pass that examination also and open the way to the three-year divinity course that lay ahead. Higher mathematics enigmatically proved a stone of stumbling. Despite my best efforts, my self-tutoring provided me with yet another compensatory Ordinary pass instead of the requisite Higher pass. Time had run out and I was reconciled not to be seeking the qualification of Licentiate in Theology by the conclusion of my course. I would study all the set subjects but I would not present for the final qualifying examination. Provided I passed all university class examinations I would emerge, being a mature student, as a Licensed Minister of Religion that had ever been my aim.

At a personal and social level my second year in Pre-Divinity had deepened friendships and had also led to new-found ones. Because of the vagaries of the academic system, our small friendship circle was increased by the addition of two new friends in particular. Andrew McPhail and Sandy McDonald joined us and further variety was added to the qualities and interests that we all instinctively displayed when together. Drew McPhail brought with him dry wit and steady good humour. He had an encyclopaedic knowledge of films and the film industry. He hailed from Irvine and I detected that he probably had, in common with myself, a not too easy upbringing. I liked him instantly and enjoyed his company. Sandy McDonald was another warm, likeable young man who, as with Drew McPhail, was about three years my junior. Sandy had been born and brought up in Bishopbriggs but his Church life had been focussed more recently at St George's Tron Church in Glasgow, which had been achieving great things under the guidance of the charismatic evangelical ministry of Tom Allan, who represented the very acceptable face of evangelicalism. Sandy McDonald had required no persuasion in this regard and owned Tom Allan as a dear friend and mentor in much the same way as I had regarded Dr Steven. Sandy had been aspiring to management in the field of timber technology and had been in the employment of Brownlee & Sons Ltd, a large timber merchant in Glasgow. He was, therefore, another man who would be bringing to the service of the Church a wider experience of life than was usual amongst the ministry. This common background was, no doubt, one influence that drew us together in friendship.

On the domestic front, Rena was kept busy with the multifarious tasks associated with motherhood. Douglas and Gillian remained delightful and our home was an extremely happy one. During the summers of 1964 and 1965 my former employers were most generous in allowing me to return to the office and lend a hand in ways that were mutually beneficial. I received a decent salary over the four summer months of the long annual university break, and this extra income, added to a very generous award from the Scottish Education Department, meant that we managed most comfortably indeed. This pattern of relative financial ease was to be maintained for the entire duration of my five-year course. Rena assisted over this period by obtaining, as a pharmacist, locum work for two hours each evening on two nights per week. This may appear little but her salary was sufficient to cover the cost of our monthly mortgage payments and was of great assistance. My wife was enabling me to devote myself entirely to study without having to be concerned with the financial side of our affairs.

Chapter Two

Early in October 1965 I embarked on my first of three years' study towards the ministry. Our lectures at a time of great change at Glasgow University remained focussed on the Department of Theology, which had been transferred from the historic buildings it had occupied for so long to more suitable and more modest accommodation located nearby. A good many of our lectures continued to be taken at Trinity College. Walking exercise was, therefore, written into our script each day. The divinity course involved five disciplines, namely: systematic theology, practical theology, New Testament, Old Testament and ecclesiastical history. To assist us in our assimilation we had a rich variety of professors and lecturers well qualified for their task.

The Department of Systematic Theology boasted two professors. Gregor Smith was a cultivated man with an incisive mind, but he remained somewhat remote. Ian Henderson occupied the other chair in theology and he was a most immediate and pleasant man who, nonetheless, was engaged in quite a bitter war with the Church establishment, as testified to in the name of his acclaimed book *The Power and the Glory*. He was resentful of power politics in the Church and he wished to have his say. He sustained his lectures despite being severely incapacitated by a set of lungs that barely functioned because of the ravages of ill health. We all had considerable respect for him.

The man engaged in the task of honing and refining us as ministers was the legendary Murdo Ewen Macdonald who had made his name as a challenging and compelling preacher during his ministry at St George's Edinburgh. I found him hugely impressive as a preacher and amazingly dull as a lecturer. Murdo Ewen was a man of impeccable integrity and honesty. Whilst he displayed his left-leaning political views for all to see, and whilst he was intolerant of any but state education, he was totally disarming in personal conversation. His character and manners were his best and most profitable teaching instruments.

Another giant of the 20th century Church oversaw the New Testament Department. Professor Willie Barclay had more the appearance of a genial butcher than that of an academic. He was a bluff pleasant man who had, of course, gained worldwide recognition and acclaim for the unending stream of books which flowed from his pen. As a lecturer he was absolutely top class. He had a wonderful knack of recapitulating as he went on, and note-taking from him was always a pleasure and never a chore. His main relaxation centred on his leadership of the Trinity College Choir which, under his baton, travelled very widely and was always well received. The choir always carried a number of comedians whose contributions added to the repertoire and always gave their performance a special frisson of pleasure. I, having absolutely no musical ability, could not offer for membership and I suspect Professor Barclay, if he could be faulted on this count, paid slightly more attention to those who identified with his choir.

The Dean of the Faculty and Professor of Old Testament Studies was John Mauchline, a granite-featured man of fine presence who spoke with a clipped stentorian accent which was difficult to place but nonetheless easy to imitate, which we sometimes mischievously did. Nor was it inappropriate that he was nicknamed 'Yahweh' – the God of the Old Testament. Professor Mauchline had not the international repute of some of his colleagues but he communicated his subject with clarity and occasionally with telling dry wit.

Professor Foster, an academic down to his bootstraps, headed ecclesiastical history. He was interested in the minutiae of the subject under consideration and was possessed of a rather crusty manner. None of us ever felt particularly close to him. He would waft into our presence and then silently slip away. It could not be said that he infused great light into what could sometimes be a dullish subject.

With these men at the helm, our academic study was varied and interesting. It was noticeable, particularly in the class of systematic theology, that an element in the class, students having conservative evangelical tendencies, was sometimes discomfited by the pronouncements of our professors. On one such occasion, as Gregor Smith was lecturing, one of our diehard conservatives interrupted the professor in full flow. 'Professor' he interjected, 'you may think that I am naïve but' and that was as far as he got. Quick as a flash, Gregor Smith retorted, 'Young man, you are naïve!' an all-sufficient put down.

This incident highlighted the polarities in the range of theological views to be found in our extremely large class of thirty-three students. The general consensus was that the so-called Bible-based Christians needed the insights which rigorous academic study would provide in order that they might more critically embrace and promote the faith. In the main, they could reasonably be said to be suffering from the disease of the closed mind. Their attitude to much of their academic study was that it was an assault upon them and a test of their faith. They would not give an inch and 'the sooner all this theological nonsense was behind them the better'. I, on the other hand, was operating on a largely blank canvas but I never encountered anything by way of instruction that came close to assailing my recently acquired faith. Quite the reverse, with particular reference to my New Testament studies, which tended to support and justify my previous long-held doubts concerning the nature of, and background to, so many New Testament narratives. It had increasingly seemed to me that the wheat needed to be separated from the chaff. Academically, this exercise was very much welcomed. As month succeeded month it was becoming clear to me that I was not being prepared for leadership within a homogenous Church but rather one within which there were widely diverging factions. This prefiguring of distinctions could not be wholly pleasing, and particularly so because of the absence of mutual goodwill between polarised groupings. I had not reckoned with this reality when I had been so swiftly and securely thrust into the embrace of the faith. On the credit side, the experience of these encounters would, in all likelihood, be but a reflection of the condition of the individual membership of the Church. To be forewarned was, doubtless, to be forearmed. To minister successfully, the lesson seemed to be: account had to be taken of, and due weight given to, the disparate opinions of different people.

By the early summer of 1966, I completed my first year of divinity studies, having passed all subjects most comfortably. The summer was in prospect and I had declined to continue seasonal work with Mather & Platt, and turned my mind to the possibility of pulpit supply. I had completed three years of my five-year course and I had not yet preached. This had to be rectified. Because of my limited background in the Church, I had reasoned that it would require much time and the acquiring of much greater knowledge before I could ever consider being involved in preaching the Word in the face of a congregation. Now, however, I was within two years of ordination; I had better act swiftly. Without exception, all my friends and fellow students had experience of preaching. They relied, in the main, upon obtaining pulpit supply from the lady who acted as the pulpit supply agent for Glasgow Presbytery. I contacted Mrs Brydone and without demur she arranged that I should conduct morning worship at Howwood Parish Church on Sunday 10th July at 12 noon. The minister, the Rev. John Campbell, would be on holiday that day.

In a mood of great anxiety and trepidation, I arrived at this modest little church and I was conducted with great courtesy to the small vestry. At 12 noon, for the first time ever, I issued the call to worship. I followed my meticulously prepared order of service with the utmost concentration and at about five minutes past one o'clock, I pronounced my first benediction. I had been marvellously sustained throughout and I had even taken time to note meeting eyes with a middle-aged lady who had her gaze fixed upon me throughout. As the congregation streamed out at the close, she shook me firmly by the hand and expressed her thanks for the service. I could not imagine the circumstances that she brought with her to that particular service but I did sense that she had come bearing a special need. Public worship, I required no convincing, was a most special event within which all manner of human need could be addressed and met. In my preparatory prayer, in secret, I had earnestly prayed that I might be upheld and that the gathered congregation would be served. In response, I found that, as promised, *'underneath were the Everlasting Arms'*.

I gained much needed experience by preaching to congregations in Glasgow, Roseneath, Paisley and Kilbirnie during the next two months. Following my introduction to the preaching circuit, I judged that I was catching up with my much more experienced friends. By this stage in our training, almost all the students were committed to student assistantships within local congregations; the student benefiting from the experience and wisdom of a senior minister. He would assist at public worship and occasionally conduct the entire service under the scrutiny of his 'bishop', as the senior man would be called. Opportunity would be afforded for pastoral visitation and counselling. The sick would be upheld in prayer at home and in hospital. There would frequently be an involvement too with the youth of the congregation. In return for these services the student received a nominal salary.

I took soundings amongst friends as to the best way forward. There were always a number of vacancies at the start of the new academic year and a rush by students to be settled with the most highly respected ministers. In a most surprising manner to me I found that I had been commended to no less than three most distinguished and regarded ministers in the south of Glasgow. I met with the Rev. James Munn in the first instance. Mr Munn was the quietly evangelical, scholarly minister of the business-orientated congregation of Newlands South. Almost simultaneously, I had been recommended by another fellow student, Robin Yates, to his then bishop, Dr John Kent of Cathcart South. Robin had created a strong reaction to his staunchly held Calvinist views in an otherwise liberal-minded congregation, and Dr Kent was ready for a step change in approach. In my interview with him, he came across to me as a most astute and kindly man and he indicated in the course of what was intended as a preliminary interview that he would be delighted if I would agree to be his student assistant. I pointed out that I had already met, in a preliminary manner, with James Munn. The two men were good friends and Dr Kent indicated that the proper course might be to await my follow-up interview with Mr Munn and that if he were keen on my going to him, I might reflect that he had first choice. This was graciousness at its best and I resolved to await my further interview with Mr Munn. As if this were not complicated enough, I had a call at my home that very night from the Rev. Ironside Simpson, minister at nearby Merrylee Church. He had obtained my name and sensed that he and I might get on well together. Ironside Simpson was a formidable man, of fine voice and appearance. He was ex-military and his bearing spoke of this background. He was certainly a minister of the old school and it showed by his adoption of top hat, deep clerical collar and striking white starched cuffs. I explained my predicament in detail and the fact of my meeting with his near neighbour Dr Kent that afternoon. Mr Simpson took this all in and indicated that I should not make a decision without first visiting his church and reviewing the whole scene. I was somewhat bemused by this turn of events. It would have appeared discourteous not to follow his suggestion and, upon obtaining my agreement, he insisted that we visit at that very hour. I joined him in his car and off we went. As we turned into Merrylee Road and were approaching his most impressive church complex, he cautioned me to be quiet when we stopped, and justified this strange behaviour by explaining that Dr Kent's manse was located next to his church. It would not do for us to be seen collaborating in the circumstances! Once inside the cathedral-like sanctuary, Mr Simpson raised the lights to allow me to behold the undoubted beauty of the building. He then gave me an indication of its effective acoustics by issuing a towering clarion call to prayer and invited me to follow suit. I thanked Mr Simpson for all his consideration and explained in some detail how Dr Kent had suggested I handle my happy predicament. Mr Simpson was relaxed that the matter should be handled in this way.

I met with James Munn on Wednesday 14th September and he reiterated his initial position, which was that he sensed that God would be well pleased for us to engage together in promoting the work of the kingdom. This was an argument that I was not prepared to refute, and although, of all three men, James Munn was the one I was least personally drawn to on the basis of his perceived theology, I expressed much pleasure at the prospect of becoming his assistant. As if to confirm my reservations touching on the personalities of the three clergymen in question, James Munn sank to his knees and offered felicitous prayer, seeking God's special blessing upon us in the work we would share. I had been so surprised by my new bishop's piety and posture that I failed to join him in his genuflection. Perhaps, Freudian-like, I was simply being my own man even so early in our contract.

My new guide and enabler, James Munn, was a serious-minded, learned man who presented a formidable exterior to those whom he sensed he might have to guard against. On the other hand, when in relaxed mode, he was the epitome of warmth and friendliness. He was not a man to be crossed despite the engaging smile he often displayed. He was an evangelical and most keenly committed to displaying his colours. I sensed from the very outset that we would get on well together. I was confronted by yet another worthy, honest and non-dissembling sort of man and I trusted that I would meet many more of his kind within the ministry in the years that lay ahead. I was immediately assigned to certain tasks. The Youth Circle at Newlands was numerically very strong, with membership of about seventy or so. The age range was from seventeen to twenty-five, with a good number inclining towards the latter. I was immediately appointed joint president alongside the elected president. Mr Munn sought to exercise influence and control over his largely sophisticated younger members by means of the assistant's presence and, he hoped, restraining wisdom. I was now aged thirty-one and thus young enough to slip into a leadership and guidance role without too much difficulty. I was also commissioned to take an active part in the regular Bible study group. This small group comprised mainly older and sometimes retired professional people such as doctors, lawyers and teachers, who despite their common professional background exhibited such diverse expressions of the faith that I was pleased to share their company and their fellowship together with occasional jousts on the issues under examination.

Since my dislocation with my minister in my own congregation, I had lacked the fellowship of a wise senior colleague and I now much looked forward to gaining new insights and experience from my collaboration with my new bishop. Events were to interfere dramatically with my hope. One Sunday, October 30th 1966, barely a month after my being appointed student assistant, as we were preparing quietly in the vestry ahead of morning worship, James Munn became ill. We quickly called for a doctor from the gathering congregation. It was evident that Mr Munn was in the process of suffering a stroke. He remained sufficiently alert to insist that he was all right and would conduct worship as usual. James Munn in his own domain could be intimidating and somewhat authoritarian, and the doctor was having a degree of difficulty with him. I decided that I was, perhaps, best placed to convince my minister that he could not possibly conduct worship and said so as forcibly as I could. The poor man signalled his assent and we awaited his removal from the church by ambulance. Meantime, it was almost eleven o'clock and the service was due to start. One of those crowding into the vestry was Dr Ronnie Falconer, a minister of the Church, who was at the time head of BBC Religious Broadcasting, Scotland. My immediate thought was that Dr Falconer would maybe take the service. He explained, however, that he had a past heart problem and it would not be possible for him to assist in our emergency. He asked me, however, if I had a prepared sermon at home and encouraged me to retrieve it and so stand in. Left with no option, I dashed off in my car to my home in Cathcart, located one of about four sermons I possessed, found the notes for a children's address and gathered prayers that I had used over the past summer, and sped back to Newlands Church. At about 11.35 a.m. I was conducted into the presence of a pensive and concerned congregation. I wended my way through the service in the best manner I could, given my total unpreparedness, and achieved its closure about an hour later without catastrophe. The good people of Newlands took me to their hearts as their young assistant who 'had been thrown in at the deep end' and enduring goodwill followed me throughout my two-year stay in their midst.

Chapter Three

The immediate impact of Mr Munn's illness was that I was accelerated into much more responsibility than would be usual for the student assistant. I became responsible for hospital visitation and inherited the minister's round for sick and elderly visitation. I was now required, as available, to prepare for and conduct funeral services at both a congregational and parish level. The preparatory and follow-up visits to such homes exposed me to the nature and extent of personal and family grief. I endeavoured to identify with their sadness of heart and present to them the comfort and strengthening of the faith, as I deemed appropriate. It was truly a great privilege to be allowed such free access to folk in their strickenness and need, and I found this costly ministry very rewarding indeed. It was also touching to receive letters of appreciation from families and individuals who, upon our earlier acquaintance, might have thought that their loved ones would have been worthy of more than the ministrations of a mere assistant. Without doubt I was now very clearly being prepared for what I judged would be my life's work. It can be freely acknowledged that profound mystery surrounds the interaction between life and death.

One Sunday morning, Dr Douglas, one of many general practitioners in the congregation, drew me aside and explained that one of his patients, a very aged lady, was at the point of death. She was seemingly also a fringe member of the congregation but, that apart, he thought it would be helpful to the family if I could visit her before she died. I agreed, of course, and visited the address provided. The district of Newlands comprised mostly well-maintained middle-class houses. The door was opened in response to my ring and a middle-aged, uneasy-looking woman, whom I took to be the daughter, admitted me to a dark, dingy hallway. The lady was taciturn and largely uncommunicative, but when I explained the reason for my visit she led me upstairs to another mean-looking room, reminiscent of my childhood, where lay a very old lady who was, as the doctor had indicated, very near to death. The daughter evidently wished no part in what was to follow, and without a word she left the room, leaving me with her old mother. It was not a loving scene. There I was, with limited experience of dealing with the dying and none whatsoever of this strange circumstance. How was I to bring succour and comfort to an old lady that I had never met before and who was clearly beyond all hope of ever hearing anything I might say? I was truly perplexed and felt totally inadequate. At this point I recalled the advice given me some weeks before by Dr Falconer who, in a conversation I had with him about pastoral counselling, had said, 'Remember Hugh, there is always the twenty-third psalm!' I felt into my pocket and produced my small

New Testament complete with psalms. I found the twenty-third psalm and, watching over the old lady, I intoned the psalm's memorable words. At the psalm's conclusion, I offered prayer as best I could and then I silently withdrew. I descended the stairs and as I reached the doorway the daughter appeared, opened the door and bade me goodnight. As I left that home I wondered if I would be called upon to conduct the funeral. As it happened, I received no call throughout that week. On the following Sunday morning, Dr Douglas sought me out, and with a somewhat bewildered look on his face he asked, 'What, Mr Sawers, did you do with that lady?' I, just as surprised, asked him what he meant. He explained that the old woman had been bedridden for the past three months and more recently all the evidence had pointed to her life ebbing. She had not eaten for a while and her death was imminent. However, within a short time of my leaving her house she had got up from her bed and alerted her daughter that she was hungry and wished to eat. By the end of the week after my visit she had strengthened greatly but could give no account of what had happened. Neither, of course, could the daughter who had absented herself from her mother's sickbed for the duration of my visit. I explained to Dr Douglas that my expectation for the outcome was entirely in line with his. For the record, I was not called upon to conduct a funeral from that address during my stay at Newlands South.

Mr Munn made a slow recovery and, in time, returned to his pulpit. At one point there were slight echoes of the consternation I had experienced at my former church on the vexed subject of total abstention. Mr Munn was a vehement opponent of the use of alcohol and, having a number of licensed trade proprietors within his congregation, he had a declared policy of preaching once per year on the evils of drink. In order to avoid giving particular offence to those in the trade, he always intimated his intention to preach on the subject, in advance. Anyone who would take exception to the topic could choose to be absent. Although I knew I had much to learn from my bishop, this was one policy that I would not be following. If I felt sufficiently strongly to preach on a theme like this, and I doubted if I ever would, then I would wish those to whom it applied most, to hear it. Mr Munn, despite his strongly held views, was oddly open to not wishing to distress or upset those with whom he held office. This propensity was further given evidence to in the incident I now relate.

Towards the end of my time at Newlands, the Youth Circle arranged one of a recurring number of weekends that were, apparently, among the highlights of their existence over the years. Lochgoilhead was the chosen venue during my time, and it fell to me to act as a sort of chaperon for the mixed group. All previous assistants had carried out this function. We settled in on the Friday evening, and within the organising committee we buckled down to producing a programme deemed suitable for such a group. There were to be discussions and debates on religious and current affairs, and periods of organised bible study, followed by time set aside for improvised entertainment. All of this was fine, and no doubt my predecessors had carried back to Mr Munn detailed accounts of all these activities. The dimension not reported on ever, I came to discover, was the extra-curricular activity embarked upon after lights out. The men and women were properly, in such a situation, segregated, mainly in rooms providing double occupation. I had the privacy of a single room, but the room was not sufficiently soundproofed to avoid my hearing the noises of the night. I was sufficiently discreet as not to disturb the privacy of others, but it was perfectly clear that some occupants had exchanged rooms. I was experiencing the true character of the appeal of the weekend for at least a number of our young men and women. Upon my return, my bishop, in a mood of enthusiasm, asked me how the weekend had progressed. He knew, after all, how much the event was keenly anticipated. As I reported to him, it was most obvious that this was not at all news to his liking. He found it almost impossible to think of his Youth Circle, whose fathers, in a good number of cases, were his elders or other office bearers, as being implicated in doubtful behaviour. Nor did he wish any evident action to be taken. He did not say so, but I knew that, for him, he would have preferred that I had not noticed anything untoward. I viewed the situation differently from him, and I would have sought a remedy whilst acknowledging the ever-present propensities of youth. In short, I would not have ignored the situation. That said, James Munn and I had become tethered by a bond of mutual friendship that was to grow ever stronger. I completed my second year of theology, again very comfortably, and moved on in October 1967 to my final year. I realised that after four years' intensive study I had been caught up in a cocoon separating me from so many of my former interests. I had experienced all this time at university but had devoted little attention to sporting interests. Participation in football and cricket could have happened but there had never been any time. Politics had been a lifelong interest and yet I had never popped my head into the students' union debating chamber over these four years. I had derived no benefit from the sporting and political activities associated with university life. Perhaps this was a reasonable penalty to be paid for my being a married, mature student with a single, clear focus. My goal was now, however, clearly within range.

The final year simply sped past and, into the new year of 1968, I, in common with my fellow students, turned my attention to the procedures that lay ahead of my completing my preparation for the ministry. The Presbytery of Glasgow required that I be taken on trials for licence and this was arranged to take place in February at Giffnock South Church, where the Rev. Wilf Toward was the minister. The minister's task here was to assess that the divinity student was a competent person in his conduct of public worship. Although only rarely would a candidate be failed at this stage, the occasion was one that was ever approached in a mood of trepidation and anxiety. Mr Toward was most considerate leading up to the service and complimentary after it, to my obvious relief.

Final class examinations were all that now stood between me and my proceeding to licence. The examinations presented me with distinctions in three of my five subjects and good results in the other two. Coincident with all this activity around church and university, I was looking to the prospect of securing my first charge. My assistantship at Newlands South had been of the utmost benefit in terms of preparation, and I was confident that I was now well-equipped for the task at hand, whatever and wherever that might be.

The entire final year student body had taken to scanning the press and appropriate publications to determine the number and locations of church vacancies. There was an inside route also. Our lecturers and the students themselves sometimes had access to leverage. Sandy McDonald and I had become close friends over the past two years and Sandy was aware of a vacancy within his own congregation at Bishopbriggs Kenmure. The departing minister had been another good friend of Sandy's and he had experienced a degree of personal animus from a securely placed senior office bearer. It was locally understood that the incoming minister would require gifts of determination and resolve if the congregation were not to suffer from continuing friction between the new man and the obdurate office bearer. This was hardly a scenario to fill me with joy, but the charge looked otherwise to be challenging, and Sandy thought that I had the personality and strength to be of help. My name found its way to the Vacancy Committee. I was duly heard and encouraged to visit and inspect the church to reinforce my interest. I became aware that a strong case was being presented in the direction of inviting me to become sole nominee. At this point I reflected very carefully on what I deemed to be the true nature of a call. Matters at Bishopbriggs were proceeding almost too smoothly for my liking. My interest was aroused by an advertisement in the *Glasgow Herald* concerning a vacancy in Penicuik South Church. This, I thought, was nearer the real thing. I had previously visited Penicuik some ten years before whilst on business for Mather & Platt, and the small town had not impressed me. It had looked dreary and uninviting with its serried ranks of council housing reaching down to its main street. It was not to be compared to Bishopbriggs, but did not Abraham venture where he was inclined not to? Penicuik might, after all, be the place to consider. I prepared my application two days ahead of the date for successful delivery, but did not post it immediately as I was still in a quandary as to whether or not I should proceed. My letter of application was slipped into the post box within minutes of my now self-imposed deadline. I received a most rapid response and a delegation came through from Penicuik the following Sunday. By special arrangement with Mr Munn, I was given charge of the service at Newlands that day to accommodate the needs of the Penicuik people. I was contacted immediately and asked to travel to Loanhead West Church the following

Sunday to enable the entire Vacancy Committee to witness me preach. After I had conducted morning worship, I met with the committee and was questioned at some length. One member, noting that I had not yet aspired to a clerical collar, was keen to have me confirm that I had experience of conducting funerals.

Rena being with me, we retired to the local hotel for lunch, at which point the committee felt it appropriate to invite us to return with them to Penicuik to look over the manse. We did this and, as we were returning home, we both sensed strong signals that spoke of my acceptability to them. I reported our experience with the Penicuik people to Sandy McDonald and he was able to confirm that late the previous week, the Bishopbriggs Vacancy Committee had charged their clerk with inviting me to become the sole nominee in the vacancy.

I now had the happiest of dilemmas. How should I proceed? After considerable thought I decided that the correct way forward would be to accept the first of any invitations that might be extended to me. In light of my secret intelligence, it looked most likely that I would hear from the Bishopbriggs people first. Indeed, what had happened to their invitation that it had not yet been communicated to me? My wait was soon over. Mr Willie Thompson, the session clerk of Penicuik South Church, contacted me by telephone and very graciously extended the invitation on behalf of his committee. In accordance with the position that I have outlined, I was able to thank him warmly and I accepted. Two evenings later I received what I knew to be a belated invitation from the Bishopbriggs committee clerk to be their sole nominee. I detected no great distress in the voice of the Bishopbriggs representative when I indicated that I was now otherwise committed. It came as no surprise to learn that the clerk to the Vacancy Committee was the very gentleman who, as it were, ruled the roost there, and whom my good friend Sandy McDonald had identified as the individual who might be in need of some restraining. This gentleman, although having been instructed by his committee to communicate with me all of a week before, had failed, for his own reasons, to do so. He, apparently, was the single voice on the committee who had no desire to have me called as their minister. God truly works in mysterious ways, His wonders to perform!

To heap wonder upon wonder, I leap ahead of my ordination at this point. Willie Thompson, who was to become a dear and cherished friend in all the years to come, had this to say concerning my call. 'When, Hugh, we responded to your application and travelled through to Glasgow to hear you, in the course of the service at Newlands, it came to me very powerfully that you were to be the man for us at Penicuik South.' He went on, 'It was not anything about your prayers, or your address to the children, or indeed the content of your sermon, which so convinced me. It was, rather, your reading of the Old Testament lesson, psalm no. 27!' Here, I have no doubt whatsoever, was 'deep calling unto deep'. As I was preparing for that most important service, I consciously chose to bring with me to the service a remembrance of my late, greatly loved minister, Dr Steven. My faith had been vested in the most telling and sublime of incidents, and Willie Thompson's testimony concerning his persuasion as to the rightness of my call was grist to the mill in this respect.

Beyond the invitation to become sole nominee lies the test of appearing before the vacant congregation and preaching for acceptance. All this due process was happening apace during April 1968. I had not, at this point, become a licentiate of the Church; in other words, a minister. This solemn event happened under the auspices of the Presbytery of Glasgow at an impressive service held in Glasgow Cathedral on the evening of May 2nd 1968. I was licensed that night as a preacher of the Gospel and now my doubting Vacancy Committee member from Penicuik could rest satisfied. I was now entitled to wear a clerical collar as a mark of my office. On a notable Sunday morning, May 15th, Rena and I made our way to Penicuik in anticipation of the 11.30 a.m. service and the 6.30 p.m. service; at which services I would be carefully scrutinised and thereafter voted upon. By way of a gentle introduction to my day, the clerk to the Vacancy Committee, together with his wife, had earlier communicated and invited us to visit them on our way to church in order to rest and refresh ourselves ahead of the events of the day. This invitation represented the kind and considerate nature of both who, again into the future, were to become secure, lifelong friends.

Having heard something of the background of the congregation in recent times, and a consequent need for healing and repair, I elected to take as my text for my sermon that morning a passage from the prophet Nehemiah Ch. 2, v. 17 *'Come, let us build up the wall of Jerusalem, that we be no more a reproach'*. I also conducted the evening diet of worship, and by the conclusion of the ballot on the Tuesday evening following, there voted in my favour one hundred and seventy-six, and against me, three. I was overwhelmingly now the minister elect of Penicuik South Church.

On the evening of June 11th 1968, in the face of an expectant and well-filled church, I was, with due ceremony and solemnity, ordained as a minister of the Church of Scotland and I was, that night, given into the responsibility for the care and cure of souls within the congregation and parish of Penicuik South. As a curious aside, my ordination was, as in the historic tradition within the Presbyterian polity, marked by the laying on of hands by members of the Presbytery to whom, as Church law states, it doth belong. In my case though, there was a singular deviation. Jack Beaumont, the neighbouring minister from Penicuik North Church and a keen ecumenist, had, without consultation, invited the local Roman Catholic priest, Father Jackson, and also the local Episcopal priest, to be present for my service of ordination. At the moment of ordination, these two clerics came forward and joined the assembled presbyters in the laying on of hands. I have, as a result, been well and truly ordained, even if, as was the case, the manner of my ordination provoked controversy at the following Presbytery meeting. Clarification was sought that such an incident could never occur again. Another chapter in my life had closed and I was now primed for a distinctly different route. Rena and I retired that night with a keen sense of God with us. I prayed that the phase about to open would find me worthy of my high calling.

Chapter Four

Almost the first thing that I did upon ordination to my new charge in Penicuik was to make a rapid survey of the condition of the congregation and attempt an assessment of its strengths and weaknesses. The recent vacancy had arisen with the departure of its strongly conservative evangelical minister who had become embroiled in a distressing personal situation with a young widow in the congregation. There was rawness under the surface on this count and healing would be necessary.

The congregation, I soon found, was typical of many within the Presbytery of Dalkeith, in that it was inward-looking, without ever really being aware that it was so. The members comprised mainly good-living, decent, long-term residents of the area, who were very wary indeed of a different breed of incomer to the new and growing Wimpey estate located nearby. At the point of my arrival, the Kirk Session and the Deacons' Court had been modestly infiltrated by a small number of capable and, by definition, deeply committed evangelicals, who had been drawn into membership of the congregation through the appeal of the lately resigned minister. Youth organisations within the congregation were totally absent.

The Sunday school was a modest affair. The nominal roll of the congregation numbered five hundred and ninety-two but bore absolutely no relationship to the usual nominalism within the Church of Scotland which, in a so-called healthy congregation, was measured by the accepted formula of one-third regular attenders, one-third rarely attending and one-third never attending. At Penicuik South, as was also the case generally in this part of the east of Scotland, we failed to measure up to even this modest standard, which, as a matter of opinion, I thought an indictment of the entire National Church. I was interested, of course, in discovering whether my predecessors had been much involved in what I measured as a rather sad state of affairs. My researches indicated that the inherited worshipping congregation of about a hundred was as good as it had been for a long time. My immediate predecessor had succeeded the Rev. John Laing who, I was eagerly informed, was no preacher. He could barely attract a congregation of fifty. I, from other sources, found that Mr Laing had many good qualities but had been a quiet, retiring man who had found it difficult to stir his people. His predecessor, on the other hand, evoked many memories of thoughtful and sacrificial service and an enduring sense of gratitude, particularly amongst the very elderly to whom he had ministered most sensitively and with great acceptance. This group was totally forgiving of the fact that he had altogether too much dependence on alcohol. This weakness had not endeared him to a much smaller group who took his indulgence as being totally unworthy of the 'cloth'. Many years after his ministry, he was remembered with much kindness, and the story lived on to be passed to me, whereby the minister would appear with regularity, early of a winter's morning, to light the fire of an ageing old body, too weak to undertake this task for herself. This was testimony to practical Christianity at its best and for the minister it provided a lasting testimony. I was early to discover that I shared a little of his kudos in that we both had hailed from Glasgow!

As I surveyed the pattern of past worship in our congregation, it was borne in on me that evangelism would have to proceed from within. We would require to secure inner health spiritually before we would ever be equipped to consider reaching out into our community and beyond. I had come from experiences gained with two large, thriving and notably wealthy congregations which, as part of their *raison d'être* provided lavishly towards the support of ailing and deprived congregations throughout the country. Beyond that, they also contributed generously towards the outreach of the Church abroad.

I totally acknowledged and understood that our resources were infinitely more thinly spread. It seemed our congregation took singular pride in the fact that they were self-supporting; that is, they accepted responsibility for paying their minister's stipend in full. I was about to operate in a totally new arena.

Sunday worship had to be my immediate priority. Where were the five hundred missing members? The truth was that the nominal roll had been vastly inflated over the years. It suited the purposes of some that this should remain so, because congregational viability was largely measured by the size of the nominal roll. To reduce the roll to realistic proportions was to put at risk the continued existence of the congregation. I had not been ordained into my charge to preside over its demise; rather the reverse. There was, though, an evident problem here and I would have to find an answer to it. As many as a hundred and fifty of our so-called members were beyond our reach because they were remote, but were insistent on keeping their connection, sometimes because they were related to other, more active members of the congregation. This latter connection of itself secured their inviolability but we also had hundreds more who exhibited little interest or no interest at all. How were such people to be stirred to a measurable commitment? If I did not have all the answers to these problems, I did, at least, have a stratagem to bring about change.

Both Dr Steven and the Rev. James Munn had, despite the many calls made upon them, believed in the need for strong pastoral oversight of their congregations and so did I. If the minister found time to meet individually with all his people in their homes and took time to discover something of their needs, their hopes and their fears, then a start would be made towards the forging of new bonds. But even ahead of this, I knew that my most immediate task was to meet with, and discover the strengths of, my fellow office bearers. These ruling elders would require to be put to the test; a test that would have nothing to do with their particular theological stance as such, but whether they were capable of fulfilling the sacred office to which they had been ordained. The examination was simple; did they truly love our Lord Jesus Christ and His cause, and were they comfortable and happy to be identified in attempting to extend His kingdom? The level of apathy and indifference evident in our congregation suggested to me, very forcibly, that our ship was, as it were, rudderless and would need immediate change in direction. Elders would require to find new roles; the roles for which they had been ordained, but which may not have been made clear or explicit. I would not be looking for saints, or men of vast intellect. I would hope to share the work in prospect with decent, thoughtful, kind and honourable men who wished, in the ways open to them, to promote the faith.

Against this back-cloth, I met with my Kirk Session for formal business some four months after my arrival, the summer being a fallow period for all such meetings. By this time, I had met individually, in one way or another, with all who comprised the session. Since I had been ordained in June, I felt that, although I was entitled to the usual ministerial break of a four-week holiday, I should restrict this to a fortnight. I arranged for Dr Steven's son, the Rev. Keith Steven, to conduct the two services in my absence. Keith duly did so, and had apparently been well received. There was, however, the tradition, widespread I fear, in the Church, that when the minister was away, so too was the congregation! In anticipation of this attitude I had urged my new congregation to show their loyalty by attending the two holiday services in good numbers. With my business background, I thought I would judge how seriously my people had listened to me by having a look at the offerings book for those Sundays and comparing their financial support as against the usual Sunday. By way of explanation; all contributors to the weekly free-will offering system are granted anonymity in that numbers replace names and only the official so appointed has access to both names and numbers. My interest was simply the level of our congregation's support on these two particular Sundays. What I beheld was deeply saddening and disturbing. On the first Sunday the total congregational offering amounted to between thirteen and fourteen pounds, and on the second Sunday the offering was between eleven and twelve pounds. How many people had been to church on these Sundays and how much, or rather, how little, had each member contributed? I was stunned by the paucity of my people's support, and on further investigation of the book I discovered that, since my arrival in the middle of June, over the period of two months, the usual weekly offering amounted to twenty-odd pounds. My people might have been expressing great gratitude for the presence and leadership of their new minister but their regard had clearly not influenced their financial support. The moment that my eyes rested on these sore financial statistics was a moment of awakening within me of the need for the love and honouring of our Lord Jesus Christ to be linked in some tangible and measurable way with our financial support for His cause. All my concern for Christian stewardship, which was to be an important element in my future ministry, had its genesis as I gazed in disbelief on these disheartening figures.

During my inaugural months in my new charge, I had the opportunity to become acquainted with my two neighbouring Church of Scotland ministers. Jack Beaumont has already been mentioned in connection with his involvement in my ordination. He and his wife were to become good and continuing friends in the years to follow. They had instantly welcomed us on our arrival in Penicuik in the week preceding my ordination and we had lunch with them in their manse. Jack had served as a missionary in Malawi for four years and had been minister of the North Church in Penicuik for the past three years. He was a human dynamo, ever moving and ever planning his next exploit. He was a cultured, scholarly type of man and a son of the manse; that is, his father had been a minister before him. Jack had a breezy, bright manner and some of his people, but never to his face, called him Jolly Jack! It could have been much worse. We were both around the same age and I saw no difficulty in prospect of our working closely together. The other nearby Church of Scotland minister was an entirely different proposition. He saw himself as very much the senior minister of the community and had been with his present congregation for a considerable period. He was manifestly senior in years, added to which he had the conceit of thinking that as minister of an Auld Kirk with a very large nominal membership, his status was markedly enhanced. He was very wary of a neighbouring colleague and was to become, as I was to find out, even more wary of me.

His demeanour was an early disappointment to me as I was settling down and hoping to establish good relationships all round. His was the first illustration of ministerial ill-will I was to encounter and it came very quickly indeed. Small towns sometimes suffered from parochialism, and their Churches could display signs of enmity too. The rift between the Auld Kirk, the historic Church of Scotland, and the Free Church, which had occurred in 1843, was still remembered and especially in smaller communities, despite the fact of the reunion of the Churches in 1929. My congregation happened to be the former Free Church formed in 1843. This was warfare set in the distant past and I had not the slightest interest in fanning any still-smouldering flames of resentment. Whilst acrimony was not at all welcome, I quickly came to realise that I would be required to fight my corner on behalf of my fellow parishioners in a spirit of neighbourly competitiveness. We were, for good or for ill, divided by the authority of the Presbytery into three parishes in Penicuik, with each minister and Kirk Session responsible for the pastoral oversight of their respective parishes. If any congregation fell below a viable number of communicants on the church roll, it would risk dissolution or readjustment in some form. Smaller congregations up and down the land lived in fear of the prospect of being dissolved. Penicuik had clearly marked parish boundaries dating from much earlier in the century. The consequence was that the largest parish contained about two thousand two hundred homes, the North Church parish approximately two thousand homes and the South Church barely one thousand homes. This allocation of territory had an obvious impact on the availability of potential church members. In the climate of the late 1960s with church rolls all over the country falling, it was imperative that congregations worked their parish territory to the full to preserve and, if possible, add to their numbers. Early into my ministry I found myself in Jack Beaumont's study, and Jack drew my attention to a huge wall map outlining all the homes in Penicuik and also defining the parish boundaries. Jack had flagged all the homes in the town wherein he had church members. Most, naturally enough, were located within his extensive parish area but a goodly number of his membership was also drawn from within my own parish and also that of our other colleague. This, very properly, reflected the freedom of choice of all churchgoing folk. The parish system merely limited congregations to trawling for new members from within their own boundaries. The system explicitly forbad poaching of new members from neighbouring parishes. There was to be contention in this area into the future but what I noticed particularly from Jack's wall map was the planned extensions to our parishes because of all the building development that was being undertaken in the town. Apparently, during the vacancy, proposed new parish boundaries had been outlined and agreed to by my two fellow ministers. I was now viewing the fruits of their labours. Virtually all the planned development was going to fall within their expanded parishes. My parish boundaries were also outlined to expand but into a greenfield site. I was set to inherit trees rather than people! Furthermore, my neighbouring ministers' extended parishes were clearly encroaching into what had been a fallow part of my existing parish. I was far from amused and said so. Jack Beaumont, in fairness, took my point and in time the Presbytery settled on a new delineation that was manifestly fairer to our congregation. This new settlement was to have the impact of permitting our congregation to breathe and attempt to reach out to potential new members.

Penicuik South had always been the poor relation when it came to attracting new members, and I was strongly of the view that we could hold our own in this respect. Sure enough, new applications for membership, instead of being a rarity, became commonplace. The Cornbank district within our parish became a rich source of new members, and I made it my business to welcome all new visitors to our congregation with a warmth that I hoped would prove compelling. Rather than a hundred or so at morning worship, we were finding traditionally unfilled pews regularly occupied, bringing our regular worshipping congregation to an appreciably higher number than hitherto. All of this encouraged our long-term faithful attenders who detected a new spirit in our midst. On Remembrance Sunday morning, the South Church was given the privilege of hosting the town's Remembrance Service, which was attended by members of the town council and representative contingents from all of the town's uniformed organisations. The impact was that for probably the first time in living memory the church housed a capacity congregation. This was, naturally, highly encouraging for me, but more to the point, inspirational to our regular congregation, who were thrilled to find their beloved church so fully used. Bearing in mind the financial strickenness of our congregation, I chose to preach on the need for revolutionary reappraisal on their part, so far as their financial support was concerned. This clarion call from the pulpit on my part had its origins in the events that had taken place recently in the Deacons' Court.

Since I had experienced the profound shock of our extremely poor offerings level, I was well aware that, in my terms, a severe financial crisis was looming. Apart from being a self-supporting congregation, we were required to make a contribution to what was then called the Co-ordinated Appeal. This was the fund that gave expression to our regard for the missionary outreach of the Church. I naturally believed that we should make the appropriate contribution and feel a sense of privilege in doing so. The Deacons' Court comprised a group of men ordained to that office and charged with the responsibility of raising the funds necessary for the good conduct of the financial affairs of the congregation. When it came to the Co-ordinated Appeal, the recipe was 'charity begins at home' and no matter the exhortation from the Presbytery in terms of the sum allocated to our congregation, the Deacons' Court was in the habit of voting for a nominal sum and there the matter rested. I, by virtue of my office, was chairman of the court and as such, felt obliged to give a definitive lead. I listened carefully to the treasurer's report, which was largely negative, borne out of much practice, and to the emerging recommendation that instead of the requested figure of two hundred and sixty-five pounds, the court would authorise fifty pounds which, it was claimed, was as much as we could afford. From my keenly expressed interest in the financial affairs of the congregation, I sensed that, if the will were present, for the first time in living memory Penicuik South Church could make a contribution in line with the expectations of our Presbytery and meet its allocation. I addressed the court in these terms and a number of sympathetic voices were raised in support but these were submerged by the collective 'realism' of the court that held to the view that it was unrealistic to suppose that our church could find such a sum. I then intimated to my utterly bemused deacons that for as long as I remained in the South Church, be it long or short, I was utterly committed to our meeting what I deemed a reasonable call on our Christian liberality and if the court were unable to meet this cost, then I personally would ensure that the required sum of two hundred and sixty-five pounds would be met in full. A stunned silence followed. Then a voice was raised in protest that they could not possibly allow their minister to meet this cost himself (my stipend amounted to one thousand and fifty pounds per annum) and he was immediately followed by one of the stalwarts of the congregation, Andrew Graham, who took out his wallet and produced a five pound note which he placed on the table. Thereupon, the treasurer himself, Alex Simpson, produced ten pounds to join Andrew Graham's donation. At which point it was moved and resolved that the whole matter be returned to the treasurer who would discover by which means he could procure the entire sum to meet our allocation and prevent their minister from having to find this money on their behalf. The outcome, and it was to prove to be a catalyst, was that by the year's end the treasurer was able to meet the allocation in full from congregational givings, and report also a small surplus on the congregational account. Moreover, Penicuik South Church, for the first time ever since the formation of the Co-ordinated Appeal, not only met its allocation but, thanks to the two donations generated from the heat of our Deacons' Court meeting, actually exceeded it. I had good reason to believe that new life and a new spirit was beginning to pervade our church affairs. By the end of 1968, evidence in this direction was gathering.

I had been quite disconcerted on my arrival at Penicuik to discover that uniformed youth organisations simply did not exist within the congregation. This situation pointed out one obvious difficulty in the way of recruitment to the congregation. I set about changing this culture and obtained the Kirk Session's early approval of the formation of a Boys' Brigade Company. I contacted Brigade headquarters and secured their cooperation and approval. I was, in the first instance, designated captain of the new 2nd Penicuik Company Boys' Brigade, although I had future officers in mind. We intimated enrolment to the proposed junior section, under the leadership of Mr James Johnston, and on the first night four young lads were recruited, including my own son, Douglas. In no time at all the section had more than twenty boys. The time was now ripe to create a company section and this rapidly happened under the leadership of one of our recent new members, Mr David Ross, who had previous Brigade experience in the west of Scotland. I passed on the responsibility of captain to David and he, with the early assistance of Bill Goodall as his lieutenant, made remarkable strides in the promotion of the company at both junior and senior levels.

Brownies and Guides were next on the agenda for formation. Here again we found a rich vein of leadership support from within the congregation. Sheila Landels, with the help of my wife and Barbara Hunter, became responsible for forming our new Brownie pack and here again the manse family produced a new Brownie in Gillian, our daughter. Meanwhile, Lyn Kinloch, yet another new recruit to the congregation, who had recently moved from the west, was the driving force behind the establishment of the South Church Guide Company. By the conclusion of 1968, the church roll had edged up to six hundred and two, and in the last six months of the year we had attracted almost all the thirty-four new members added.

Chapter Five

I was finding immense reward within my ministry and I had made a determined start on a rigorous programme of district visitation which, I realised, would occupy me for at least two years. I had immediately implemented a very full programme of elderly and sick visitation and I well understood that this would be constantly unremitting. Largely on this particular front, I won the goodwill of the static long-term element of our church population. This was ministry as they understood it and felt their elderly deserved. Having clarified the matter of our parish boundaries, the time was ripe to harness the eagerness and willingness of our most committed members towards outreach. The Kirk Session approved of a scheme of visitation into the newly built houses in Cornbank where, I was in no doubt, we could ignite interest in our church. We prepared our visitors, prayed over them and sent them out, in good biblical fashion, two by two. Our fine team of highly motivated and essentially nice people reaped a rich harvest as testified to in their reports. We saw a stream of new faces at worship and further opportunities for visitation by me opened up in response to potential new members indicating a desire for a visit. I was not losing sight of our so-called 'dead wood'; those whom the

Angel Gabriel himself could not have roused. My inherited Kirk Session was almost entirely composed of indigenous Penicuik men. Three so-called incomers were the exceptions who also represented a disproportionate resource in terms of ability, commitment and spiritual awareness. They knew assuredly the nature of their office as elders and why they embraced it. This could not be said of a fair number of other elders. For some of them, one sensed, religion did not rate too highly in the order of priorities. They had been invited at some point in the past to become elders and for reasons best known to each, had agreed. Decent, good men they so often were, but these credentials did not of themselves suffice against the claims of the office of the eldership. However, no one had apparently thought to challenge them on this ground. The question arose as a consequence: how could such a group of often unthinking men prove a potent instrument in promoting the cause of Christ? Growth in the faith, as with growth in grace, is so often intangible but nonetheless necessary if spiritual progress were to be made. It was urgent that we make such progress.

My approach with my elders was firstly to befriend them. I had no ambition to fall out with any of them. Secondly, I saw no reason why I should not challenge them when they manifestly failed to perform the function of their office. I expected my elders to have an appetite for regular attendance at public worship. Hitherto, a number of them sat lightly to that aspect of their office. Conjoined with this, I thought it not unreasonable for a ruling elder to be present at the Kirk Session meetings, when he was not otherwise prevented from doing so. Edge was added to my particular concern here because I had been made aware from my first weeks in the community that a goodly proportion of my fellow elders were also members of the Masonic Order. I further discovered that they well understood the obligations such membership reasonably imposed and that they appeared not to have any difficulty in accommodating these. Our session clerk, Willie Thompson, who was to become a dear and lifelong friend, was quite hurt when he took early soundings of me concerning whether or not I might become a member of the craft and I had to respond negatively. In this I was making no judgement as to the merits of free masonry or otherwise. I was merely making clear that I had an all-consuming calling which allowed no space for this other activity. If my fellow elders believed that they could be good Masons and good elders, that was splendid. I simply wanted to see that they were good elders and the indications on this count were not always auspicious. However, in friendship with them, I laid before them the basic criteria that would afford them to offer acceptable service, and to their credit my counsel was mainly received with seemly good grace. The eldership within our congregation was slowly taking on new meaning. This was no fanciful false imagination on my part. I guided the Kirk Session to the need for meaningful district visitation to occur during the elder's pre-Communion call. I had no desire for the continuance of the practice of elders acting as 'celestial postmen' with cards being deposited surreptitiously into letterboxes and this act being deemed a visit. This unworthy practice, where it occurred, had to stop as this represented negative visiting in the extreme and the correct approach would instead open, quite literally, doors of opportunity. Our Kirk Session adopted the procedure whereby elders would report on their district visitations to the session, highlighting individuals or families who were detached from us for whatever reason. Thus our concern became real and the particular difficulty identified. Along this route, I was convinced, lay the spiritual strengthening of our kirk.

As 1969 drew to a close, there was much for which to give thanks to God. Our Sunday school was strengthening and new teaching staff had come forward. Our recently established uniformed organisations were providing teaching and training and recreation for a good many youngsters who were developing an attachment to their church. Worship was being increasingly well supported and the elders' new confidence was being translated into a new-found appearance of members to Communion.

By the end of the year there had been a vast influx of new members to our kirk of just over a hundred. This unprecedented upsurge in membership allowed me freedom in tackling the seemingly impossible task of dealing with members who declined to worship and who failed to respond to their elder's promptings concerning presence at Communion. Until now there had never been a sufficient movement of new members into the church fellowship, which permitted the Kirk Session sufficient freedom to challenge these backsliders without putting the existence of the congregation in peril. I saw our situation in Penicuik South as a possible pattern to assist the wider Church in its battle against apathy and drift. To succeed, however, meant that the Church's ministry and eldership would need to take the battle for hearts and minds into the homes of our people as never before.

As I relaxed for a brief few days with my wife and family at Crieff Hydro, courtesy of the generosity of the Meikle Trust, which underwrote most of the short-break costs, I was able to meet up with my former fellow students. In the full flush of our early ministry we would exchange our respective experiences and our hopes and aspirations for our people. I realised quickly that some of my young fellow ministers were already encountering difficulties in various ways that were causing them anxiety. Some were in difficulty already because of their hardline evangelical zeal, which canny congregations had already, in some measure, opposed, to the discomfort of the ministers involved. Others again appeared to have no great appetite for pastoral visitation which, in some cases, was a symptom of their uneasiness with personal encounter. I began to understand that my assessment of how we could, together, work to improve the health of our congregations up and down the country was not something into which they would readily buy. They did not appear confident that, even if they wished, they could move their Kirk Sessions in the manner I had shared with them. Thus I received meagre confidence from my own little focus group that the condition of the wider Church could be radically changed. This lack of confidence amongst my fellow ministers I found truly disturbing.

My discomfiture in the condition of the Church at large was further reinforced through my involvement with my Presbytery of Dalkeith. I had been appointed as Convener of the Presbytery Youth Committee and my task was broadly to oversee and report on the health or otherwise of Christian youth education within the thirty-two congregations which comprised the Presbytery. I reported to my assembled fellow members that there had been a quite catastrophic drop in numbers attending Sunday school over the previous five years and unless remedial action was taken, the National Church would, in short order, be in obvious decline. It was becoming ever clearer that we in Penicuik South were swimming against a strong running tide.

The tide, furthermore, against which we sought to prevail was not always external. A truly odd and totally sad situation had arisen on the back of our Sunday school expansion. We found ourselves in the happy position of having to open a further Sunday school department located in the primary school within our Cornbank parish area; our restricted church hall premises could not cope with the increased number of children seeking to attend. Sometime after this new department had been established, the school premises became temporarily unavailable and we sought authority to accommodate our pupils in the nearby high school. A difficulty arose because the high school was located within a neighbouring parish. We wrote to the appropriate Kirk Session seeking their acquiescence to our Sunday school operating for a short time at the high school. We received an astounding reply from the minister and Kirk Session saying, in essence, 'We note your request to operate your Sunday school from premises within our parish and we sympathise with your problem because we too have a large Sunday school. Accordingly, we have to refuse your request.' This was monstrously unbelievable. How could a neighbouring Kirk Session, with absolutely no cause shown, act in this way? I was learning daily the complexities of Church fraternity.

This uncooperative letter demanded a response and I realised that the only way forward was through procedures available in Presbytery. Our Kirk Session reported our concerns to our governing body, and in due course the minister involved and myself were called before the appropriate Presbytery committee who heard our evidence and passed judgement. Suffice to say the committee rebuked the implicated Kirk Session and its minister and ordered that free access be given immediately to our displaced Sunday school.

That such an incident could happen between two congregations committed to the same cause was positively distressing. I was deeply saddened also that a fellow minister should have been exposed to so open a rebuke. Personality clash, if it could be so-called, had raised an ugly head.

Within our congregation, 1970 progressed exceedingly well, and I derived much strength from the reports reaching my ears, both from casual visitors and from intending new members, that what attracted them most on our corporate worship was a keen sense of the Spirit in our midst. A congregation that could evoke that kind of response had to be operating in the right manner. To further cement our growing as a caring, outgoing congregation, we established visitation teams to help meet the needs of our elderly. My own aged and infirm list was in excess of a hundred and occupied a good deal of my time, but lay visitation and neighbourliness, and offering help with transport, was an added dimension of care. At the conclusion of the year, one hundred and nine new members had been drawn into our fellowship and further resort was made to the supplementary roll that as a result was increased by thirty-four. Despite our community being quite fluid with considerable coming and going, we ended 1970 with a greatly rejuvenated roll of seven hundred and ten members. Membership of the congregation was coming to mean more to our members than ever before.

We were in good heart at the beginning of 1971. Our Kirk Session had been much strengthened by the ordination of additional elders and by the admission of a number of elders who, having been ordained within their previous churches, brought the weight of that disparate experience with them. They quickly melded into a strong cohesive force and went about their work with conviction.

Representative of the new resources available to us was the McRae family. Douglas and Helen had settled recently in Penicuik with their two young sons and, being the thoughtful couple they were, they very properly visited the neighbouring congregations before settling on the South Church. Douglas McRae was a quiet, totally unassuming young man in his mid-thirties. He was a sensitive, caring and transparently honest man who hailed from Prestwick initially but who had returned recently to Scotland after a goodly spell in Cookstown in Northern Ireland where he had pursued his career as a research engineer. He was a boffin and, true to the stereotype, he had the reputation of being somewhat absent-minded. He was a truly fine man and his decision to throw in his lot with the South Church was one that was to prove of inestimable value to the congregation in the years to come. As if Douglas's added qualities of character and industry were not sufficient, in Helen, his wife, came a full flow of assets. Helen was Welsh by birth but clearly had the good sense to marry a Scot. She had seemingly endless energy and a vast enthusiasm for the promotion of Christ's cause in our midst. Fineness of character defined Helen who was ever pleasant in her manner and instant in making friends. She and Douglas together were supreme ambassadors for Christ in our midst and neither of them would I want to describe as pious. The Presbyterian faith needed many more like them. Currently, however, we had them, together with many other fine exemplars of the faith, and in that our fellowship was greatly enriched. Rena and I owned Douglas and Helen as dear friends.

My pastoral work was naturally ongoing with the usual work associated with baptisms, weddings and funerals, where in all cases I prepared in meticulous detail with visitation and interview as imperative. Visitation of the sick and dying was always a matter for tender thought and prayer, and whilst this vital ministry took a toll, however momentarily, it also provided some of the most rewarding aspects of ministry. One incident serves to illustrate this truth. One of my dearest old ladies in the congregation was Mrs Graham, whose life was ebbing to its end. We all admired the open, lovely simplicity of her faith that had characterised her entire life. She had been a member of the South Church since childhood and she had a thirst for all things touching on the faith, which meant that she was ever in her place in church on Sunday and she attended all possible weekly church groups; the Women's Guild and the like. Having done all that, she would find time to attend mid-week meetings of the local Salvation Army. Mrs Graham was a sparkling example of all that was good about the Christian faith. She shared the home of her daughter Lilias and her husband Cameron Inglis, who was an elder, and her granddaughter Zena made up the family. Lilias, not unexpectedly, was another sweet and gracious lady who had to contend with uncertain health. Cameron, her husband, was also a fine God-honouring man who was very much incapacitated, suffering as he did from emphysema. I had visited the home regularly as Mrs Graham gradually weakened, and when it became obvious that the end was very near, Lilias undertook to call me if her mother was sinking. When the call came to me, it was against the background whereby Mrs Graham had been unable to accept even liquids for the previous three days. As I reached the house, and was let in by Lilias, I met the Salvation Army captain coming down the stairs. He had heard of Mrs Graham's condition and had made a spontaneous call, which was to be particularly appropriate. Mrs Graham was being well-ministered to right up to the end. Lilias guided me upstairs and led me to the bed where Mrs Graham lay comatose. She gently soothed her mother's brow and left me to my task, which was not difficult. I clasped Mrs Graham's hand in mine and gently prayed; recalling in God's presence a life which had so enriched the community and, above all, the family, to which, even to the end, her presence had been a comfort and support in their respective needs. I then commended her to the care and keeping of a good and gracious God. I concluded my prayer and withdrew, indicating to Lilias that I would be immediately available on confirmation of her mother's death. Two hours later I had a call from the family to say that upon my departure Lilias had gone upstairs to assess her mother's condition. Mrs Graham opened her eyes and asked for a drink of water. The astounded family telephoned the doctor and upon examination the ambulance was called. Mrs Graham was transferred to hospital. Two days later I called at the Deaconess Hospital in Edinburgh and was ushered into her presence. She had not expected me and was momentarily upset that her dentures were not in place. When this was rectified, I was vastly interested to hear from a new, very alert Mrs Graham how she had been recently. This is what she told me. 'I had a dream, Mr Sawers, in which I thought I was leaving this world, when I heard a voice suggesting that perhaps my work in this life was not yet over and that maybe God still had something more for me to do, and I rallied to that thought and here I am!' And so she was! Mrs Graham recovered and was soon back on her feet, back at her place of worship, and doing all she could to help about the house in the midst of her family. Her story was to unfold even more into the future.

On a quite unrelated matter, I was to be engaged in another area touching on controversy. Two of my highly regarded and spiritually sensitive elders indicated that they wished an appointment with me at my convenience. I arranged for them to visit the manse almost immediately. The pair represented a formidable combination touching on matters of the faith and, as I anticipated their arrival at the manse, I knew the interview would be meaningful. I was by no means disappointed. They began by reciting my virtues. They were keen to acknowledge that the congregation had progressed considerably under, as they stated, my able ministry. There was just one blemish, as their spokesman put it. My ministry was insufficiently Christocentric. I seemed to be too much taken by God the Creator and had not sufficiently emphasised the work and merits of Christ the Redeemer. Now this, of course, was a point of view and I listened most carefully. It was indicated that with greater emphasis on Christology my sermons would have greater appeal. My other office bearer, by his presence, was doubtless upholding this point of view. I responded that we were each individually the end product of our own peculiar spiritual journey and that of itself would determine the nature and expression of our belief. I had been most powerfully and persuasively led into the faith and I could not arbitrarily adopt a position not in accord with my experience. I knew by whom I was called and my ministry would remain consistent with the challenges that call had disclosed. In a word, my ministry was my ministry and I would remain loyal to it. I went on to explain that I heard their concerns but could not accommodate them. My ministry would proceed along the lines my ordination permitted. In summary, I was being invited to adopt a theological position which was alien and which, at its very heart, I deemed inappropriate for the needs of a questioning society. I would minister according to my own lights. The interview was over and my visitor friends withdrew having stated their case. Despite our differing positions we were to remain secure and close friends.

As the summer approached, Rena and I decided that we

would take our four-week holiday in France. Having bought a touring caravan two years previously, our summer breaks had been spent touring around Scotland. My reputation for pastoral diligence had backfired from the very beginning of my ministry, in that Willie Thompson, my session clerk, thought that I should be kept informed of any bereavements that had occurred during my holiday; the hope being that I would return and deal with the family's needs. We had thought to escape this iron grip by resorting to touring but Willie suggested that I phone back on appointed days so that he might pass on any developments. Rena was not at all thrilled by these potential shadows hovering around our holiday. In contrast, if we were holidaying in France, we would be beyond reach, and Jack Beaumont, with whom I had a reciprocal arrangement, would attend to any needs arising.

Throughout the three years since my arrival in Penicuik I had worked at fever pitch without ever realising it. Virtually every minute of my time had been devoted to developing and improving the condition of our congregation. Constant visitation, be it with a view to bringing comfort to the needy or involving discussion to help overturn doubts or misgivings about the church, all added to the usual workload of immediate duties and calls on my time. By June I felt utterly exhausted and could barely wait for my approaching holiday, ahead of which was the annual summer fete. This was the all-important and traditional fundraising event of the year. We had made the manse garden available for the fair and this gesture was enthusiastically received and gave even greater impetus to the efforts of all involved. When the Saturday for the fete arrived, there was intense bustle and activity all over and around the manse and, of course, I was in there, as they say, doing my bit. The difficulty was that I felt awful, and apparently I looked dreadful. The reports of the day have it that I simply looked green. Our next-door neighbour, Dr Baldwin, although not a member, had opened his very impressive garden for a competition of his own devising as his contribution to our fundraising. He took one look at me and despatched me to bed. Our own doctor was called, but I explained that I was primed ready to set off for France and that the relaxation would soon put me right. The dubious GP agreed to my travel plans but insisted I appear for a consultation on my return. In the meantime, he produced a sealed letter to be passed on to the medical authorities should anything go wrong whilst I was away. A week later we loaded all our requirements, including a vast amount of tinned and packet food to sustain us for a month in France. When it came to hitching the caravan to the car I appreciated for the first time how physically weak I had become. I simply could not raise the caravan connecting assembly on to the receiving ball cap arrangement fitted at the rear of the car. I had to call on Douglas, my nine-year-old son, to assist me in securing the caravan to the car. Thereafter I coughed and spluttered at the wheel of the car all the way to France with my long-suffering family, putting a brave face to the whole scene. On reaching France we met up with friends from the congregation and their two children at Cayeux on the coast, some forty kilometres beyond Calais. The weather was glorious and the two families enjoyed a week together before, as previously agreed, we moved on to our prospective different destinations. I had spent the entire first week barely moving from around the caravan, but I felt sufficiently strong to contemplate our planned move towards Paris. We made the journey successfully and were fortunate to find accommodation at the Paris International Camping and Caravanning Site by the Bois de Boulogne. Within a few days of being settled there, my strength returned and for the remainder of our holiday I was as fit and active as ever. My holiday had provided a rest cure just as I had hoped. On my return I visited the surgery as had been arranged. My own doctor was not on duty and his replacement for the day greeted me airily with a description of symptoms entirely unrelated to my condition. He had clearly confused cases and I assured him that whatever had been my problem a month ago, I was now as fit as a fiddle and did not feel the need for any further interest. In the same mood of indifference I detected at the outset, he agreed, and I was off to be about my business. On returning to Penicuik from holiday, I took an early opportunity to thank Doctor Baldwin for his help on the day of the fete. He acknowledged that I now looked well indeed but on that Saturday he had no doubt but that my condition spoke to him of pneumonia.

I was well pleased to reflect that although I had been laid

low for a period of about five weeks, I was merely out of my pulpit for health reasons on one Sunday. Soon all the autumn activities were back in place and church life was as busy as ever.

Chapter Six

Ever since that notable day very early in my ministry when I discovered the paucity of our offerings level, I had not failed to impress upon my people the need for a level of giving which was not insulting or dishonouring to the cause we espoused. Conservative evangelicals often took pride in their allegiance to the veracity of scripture and their acceptance of its disciplines. They were familiar with the concept of tithing and frequently claimed to embrace it. Now we in Penicuik South had an inherited leavening of conservative evangelicals, but it was interesting to me to note that there was not the merest evidence of tithing in our congregation. I was not, in terms of biblical evidence, tied to the concept of tithing but as an individual expression of my love for, and dedication to, the cause of Christ, I did not have difficulty in so arranging our financial affairs, with the full and warm support of Rena, that we offered ten per cent of our earned income to the church. We did so because we believed the cause was worthy and also because I would be leading my people to express their commitment, in this as in many other ways, more fully. In which case I should be properly equipped to lead and be secure from any sniping on this count.

As I reviewed my congregation's and the Presbytery's level of support for outreach, these two facts emerged. Of the thirty-two congregations within our Presbytery in 1968 upon my arrival, Penicuik South's position was third from the bottom. The Presbytery of Dalkeith, on the same test, registered fifty-ninth place out of sixty presbyteries in the Church. These statistics appalled me. I communicated to our people the plight of our congregation, as I saw it, and insisted that surely the slightest of our aspirations had to be that we should at least be average. Whether to please their minister, or simply with a new awareness of the facts, Penicuik South Church began to show evidence of greatly increased generosity. Coincidental with that, their ability to look outward and support others in need became more pronounced. I had been active in Presbytery also on the theme of Christian stewardship and I gave vociferous support to the ageing but gentlemanly Rev. Erskine Fraser, the Presbytery Stewardship and Budget Convener. We were soon to see stirrings of a reborn willingness to identify with the need for much more informed generosity towards the Church.

As Presbytery Youth Convener, one of my responsibilities was to serve on the board of management of Carberry Tower, which had been gifted to the Church by the Elphinstone family. It was a very imposing former country house located in countryside near Musselburgh and was a centre for youth training and lay leadership within the Church and also with good residential accommodation. This extensive property was set in a large acreage of ground and its upkeep was a constant concern. The board of management was headed by, in my time, the Countess of Mar and Kellie, known as Pansy Mar to her friends. She headed up an impressive sounding board of Scottish aristocrats, such as the Duchess of Sutherland, Lady Primrose and Chairman of the Bank of Scotland at the time, and other such captains of Scottish commerce and industry who also happened to have Church sympathies. I was quite taken to be numbered in the company of these high-flying and aristocratic Scots, and little would they have known of my background as we assembled for our occasional meetings. At one such meeting, the Countess had called upon me to open with prayer and, as we sat gathered around the huge polished table, a small folded piece of paper was flicked right across the table by one of our distinguished company. I opened the paper and there before me was the cryptic message, 'I see we share a tie!' My immediate emotion was one of bewilderment instantly turning to embarrassment. I gazed down at my tie; it had a dark blue background, with diagonal narrow stripes involving, I think, red and green, and possibly white. The point was that my companion across the way seemed to think that his was the same. I thought furiously. I wondered about the Royal Navy and I considered also the Royal Navy Reserve. Could these be wavy lines on his tie rather than the straight ones on mine? Was I wearing a tie to which I was not entitled? How had I got into this mess? On reflection I knew the answer to that question! Just months before, at the

Women's Guild sale of work, I had gallantly paid the asking price of fifteen pence for the tie, which just happened to catch my eye. Now I was in a hole. I caught the eye of the gentleman involved and slightly shook my head in feigned disavowal of any possible similarity in our ties. I was glad of the distance separating us across the table and I was busily working out how, at the end of our meeting, I would be able to escape without his catching up with me. I did manage to exit the meeting without having to explain my embarrassing predicament involving a Women's Guild stall and a fifteen pence bargain. The old school tie brigade would not have been amused!

We continued to filter a stream of new members into the church and the Kirk Session remained diligent in its attempt to win disaffected long-term members back within our fold. We were more and more able to apply the sanction of the supplementary roll when all other reasonable efforts failed to evoke a response. By December 1971, another hundred members had joined us and ninety-one had left us through death, removal or, in the case of fifty-three, by transfer to the supplementary roll. What was happening in our congregation, I knew, was not being replicated elsewhere in our Church and this awareness brought its own sadness because, above all else, our Kirk in Scotland needed renewal. Our church roll was attested at 31st December as having seven hundred and eighteen in communion.

Communion was a vexed topic for some in our

congregation. I held strongly to the view that the sacrament should represent the most meaningful service in the Church calendar. By participation we could truly test the promise:

> '*O taste and see that the Lord is good*
> *Blest is the man (and the woman) that trusts in Him .*'

I had a great love of the sacrament and did not doubt that in and through it we were bound to things unseen.

> '*Here O my Lord we see Thee face to face!*'

The more narrowly-based evangelicals in our congregation had a disdain, and I could see it growing, of the constantly increasing numbers attending the sacrament. Their theological position was such that they viewed the increased response as in no manner related to their conversion, but rather the fruits of tighter administrative and disciplinary procedures, and I sensed they were not altogether happy. Their position was to misunderstand the ethos of the Presbyterian Church whereby we had the privilege of reaching out to the entire Scottish population through our system of parishes.

I well appreciated that Communion gatherings brought together quite disparate conditions of people. Some would prepare for the sacrament in a thoughtful and reverent manner. Others, again, prepared thoughtlessly and with scant regard for the significance of the act.

However, the sacrament provided the setting for interaction and had, in my view, the potential for new-found experience and spiritual growth.

I was learning that even when significant and measurable progress was being made in the witness of the congregation, not everyone was best pleased. I was soon to have evidence on this front from an entirely different direction within the congregation. I was able to write in my foreword to the congregational accounts for 1971, ahead of the congregational meeting scheduled for 29th February 1972, of the amazing transformation in the financial situation now prevailing within our kirk. The figures I reported on, in today's values (i.e. 2004), were as follows: we had been invited to contribute the sum of six thousand pounds in support of the Mission and Service Fund of the National Church. This sum would have been totally unthinkable in 1968, but it reflected in the Presbytery's view the immense strengthening of our position that had been achieved in recent years. However, the Deacons' Court had decided to provide the equivalent sum in today's money of fifteen thousand pounds from the growing fund now available. In essence, we were going well beyond the second mile in terms of generosity by providing two and a half times the required sum. This action by our Deacons' Court was unparalleled in the experience of Dalkeith Presbytery and was to have significant impact upon the other congregations within it. It was now apparent that as a Presbytery we could do immeasurably more in support of the Church than had hitherto been thought possible. Penicuik South Church was now acting as a beacon and new standards were being set.

Domestically, though, the stirrings were not all positive. A number of my elders and deacons who had served in their church for many years did not sit comfortably with the new doctrine, as they saw it, of 'giving away all their money!' At the annual congregational meeting, they found a spokesman in a long-term elder not, it has to be said, noted for his regular attendance at church or Kirk Session; work was his plea in mitigation. This elder was representative of the decent good-living men who were in office when I arrived but who lacked vision beyond the immediately parochial. This particular spokesman had a much firmer handle on matters political and it was not difficult to make the connection in the intervention that he made on his behalf and on behalf of those whom he deemed needed a voice. He rose to challenge the wisdom of supporting some aspects of the work of the Overseas Council of the Church. He declaimed that too much of our money was being sent to South Africa to support terrorists there. His credentials for speaking, so he stated, related to the fact that his son was settled in South Africa and knew the situation there first-hand which was more than we at home could claim. As chairman of the meeting I, uncharacteristically, felt rising anger. This was an attempt to undermine the goodwill and generosity of our people towards the glaring inadequacies and starvation that existed throughout the third world. Or, if it were not that, it was a blatant partisan political intervention into the realm of church affairs. Either way, this man had to be stopped in his tracks before greater mischief was let loose. I rose to my feet and responded as forcefully as I could. I explained to him that our National Church did not support directly or indirectly the African National Congress in the manner he alleged and that it was unworthy of him to make such irresponsible and inaccurate claims. I further stressed that the many good people of our congregation who had provided the funds so generously to support our outreach were pledged, by definition, to assisting the relief of hunger and poverty worldwide. His counsel, I assured him, would not have their support and so it proved. The meeting signalled its approval in the usual manner.

I was becoming aware that not only was progress on the spiritual front being questioned but also there were clear rumblings from malcontents on the financial front. My hope had to be that what we were experiencing was an expression of creative tension. At the same time I also realised that for some people the comfortable and undisturbed life is their goal. For my own part I desired that every life should be an examined one. There was wide evidence that, on this count, we still had much work before us.

My overarching desire was that with minister and Kirk Session working together, in a spirit of close friendship, trust and harmony, we would lead a congregation capable of shedding light, touching on the things of Christ, into our wider community, which would prove a blessing to that community. That, it seemed, was our reason for being.

Into the fifth year of my ministry, I was as eager as ever to take forward that plan. As the year progressed I became convinced that the fruits of our elders' informed pastoral care were becoming more evident. Church attendance had never been so buoyant and a warm friendliness pervaded the body of our people. Having said that, there remained a considerable untapped source of further strengthening of our fellowship if we could secure its release. The National Church had forever been bedevilled by the problem of nominal membership and seemingly had no answer. Membership was too often resorted to with little conviction and, once membership was attained, too little was asked in return. The three-year Communion rule, as it was understood and applied, whereby members could choose to register their continuing interest by a mere single appearance at the sacrament every three years, was an affront; no wonder we were a Church plagued by indifference and nominalism!

As I mulled over the matter of how we could awaken the inert portion of our kirk with particular reference to the sacrament, I concluded that instead of a three-year rule, a three-month measure might be more appropriate. The Kirk Session discussed the matter fully and concluded that this was a route worth travelling. We agreed a strategy whereby all identified backsliders would be noted, not by their presence, but sadly by their absence. This procedure, note, was only being implemented after the elder had frequently exhorted his charges to resume worship. After a three-month period had elapsed, the Kirk Session would have further reports on the status of the habitual non-attenders. I would also be able to contribute to the debate from my own observations. This would not be as difficult as might be imagined. From my first days at Penicuik I had an awareness of who was present at worship and by implication who was not. At the beginning, with much sparser congregations, I acknowledged the individual members as they left at the end of the service. I very soon acquired names that added, for me, pleasure to the encounter. As the congregation grew I had no difficulty in attaching names to the new faces. I believed strongly in the biblical notion that 'the good shepherd knows his sheep!' It was from this pastoral background that I could make a contribution to the Kirk Session's deliberations on this sensitive issue. Our intention was that we would write to all whom we identified as sitting too loosely to their obligations of membership. What we were about to implement was totally unheard of in the experience of our National Church and we wished our approach to be both sensitive and effective.

With the approach of summer, Rena and I again were persuaded that France was the place for us, but we felt that the caravan was somewhat cramping and, moreover, the French climate was so appealing that a large continental-type tent would suit us better, giving more space and also allowing the travel to be more relaxing without the need for towing. We had a fine holiday, and by its end I was more than ready for the incoming season's work.

From time to time throughout my ministry I have been presented with experiences that spoke, according to my understanding and interpretation, of 'deep calling unto deep'. I have long been convinced that the God who has intervened so decisively in the affairs of mankind through the redeeming work of His Son our Lord Jesus Christ, continues so to do. I have in mind the realm of faith healing within which too often resides the charlatan and the misguided. There will always be a large susceptible and gullible group within society which may be easily led and subsequently harmed by the confident claims of some so-called healers. My message has ever been: beware all such. What mystery was involved in the incident I now relate?

One of my members had quite suddenly taken ill. This lady was a very sweet and gentle person who had suffered the ill effects of recurring headaches over a long number of years. She had been removed very hurriedly to the Western General Hospital in Edinburgh, and her husband, a fellow office bearer, had telephoned me, in a state of controlled anxiety, to advise me that his wife was extremely ill and had been diagnosed with a brain tumour. I responded and visited the dear lady in hospital. I found her in a small ward accommodating herself and three other ladies. The patient managed a welcoming smile of greeting but she was naturally very apprehensive indeed. We spoke for a little and I avoided reference to the information that her husband had disclosed to me, but I knew that she was aware of her predicament. As was normal in the circumstance of a hospital visit, I concluded my time with her in prayer. We clasped hands and I spoke of the wondrous work and sacrifice of our Lord and the singular example of courage and forbearance that He had left with us. In the power and strength of the invoked Holy Spirit I prayed that her wellbeing be given into His care and love and that His most gracious will, and not ours, be done. I gently kissed her and took my leave. I was soon to hear from a totally elated husband that there had been an extraordinary development. My visit, the patient reported to her husband, left her with a sense of profound peace. The news her husband was so excited and thrilled to pass to me was that further tests had failed to show up the earlier diagnosed tumour. He indicated that the doctors were completely baffled. Husband and wife, for their part, were convinced that I had been greatly used in this incredible healing process.

Who knows the true nature of the forces at play in this particular case? Was there ever a tumour in the first place? The doctors certainly thought so! However, they could have been wrong. If they had been wrong, what was the nature of the lady's illness? Could it have been stress – or anxiety-induced? What was not in doubt was that this woman was clearly ill, and then, without benefit of drug-directed help, or any other medical or surgical intervention, she had recovered. Prayer was an element present in her time of need. Its place in her recovery belongs to the realm of faith, and those of us who attest and believe in its efficacy. There I rest the case, save to say that in the intervening thirty years that gracious lady was spared in good health to be a blessing as a much-loved wife, mother and grandmother and continued to witness a good confession.

Chapter Seven

By September, the Kirk Session finally deliberated on the perceived circumstances of those many members that we had identified for further challenge. The result was that the session clerk and myself had to append our names to no fewer than one hundred and sixty-eight letters to members whom we felt were showing little enthusiasm for their membership on the count of attendance at worship. The letter took this form:

> The Session House
> 20th September 1972

Dear...

It is with much regret that the Kirk Session notes that you have not found it possible to maintain your membership of the congregation at a satisfactory level of personal commitment.

In the circumstances, therefore, the Kirk Session now formally intimates to you its intention to remove your name/names from the roll of communicant members of the congregation.

Should you feel that there are factors that the Kirk Session should have before it, before such a decision is implemented, you are invited to communicate with your district elder, who would communicate your observations to the Kirk Session, thus enabling it to give sympathetic consideration to your case.

Please note that any representations should be made to your elder by Saturday 14th October 1972.

Yours faithfully

(Moderator)
(Session Clerk)

We expected a massive response to this communication which would, doubtless, be without precedent in the history of the Church of Scotland. I had undertaken as a matter of close pastoral responsibility, and as the prime mover in this approach, to reply to, or meet personally with, those who sought clarification. October proved to be an extremely arduous month. We received numerous letters, and I visited forty-one homes. I was particularly keen to engage with the small number who expressed outrage. This group invariably cited the so-called three-year Communion test. The words 'arrogance' and 'high-handedness' were used in a few cases to describe the action of the Kirk Session. In line with our best expectations, many of our members came to understand our position and undertook to re-examine their priorities in relation to the church. This group wished to remain with us as members. Another group decided that they should act to avoid being placed on the supplementary roll and requested their certificates of transfer. The remainder acknowledged that the supplementary roll was the place for them meantime. The outcome was that by the end of the year, forty-nine members were removed by certificate, of whom approximately twenty had been in receipt of our letter; the remainder having moved home in the course of the year. A further sixty were placed on the supplementary roll. On the credit side, we recruited seventy-one new members, notwithstanding the growing awareness in our community that membership of the South Church was not embarked upon without thought. The very much honed-down church roll now numbered six hundred and seventy-six members.

After our intensive and often exhausting pastoral supervision, I was confident that our congregation was well positioned to make a most telling witness at both congregational and Presbytery levels. Immediate evidence was forthcoming at our November Communion services when, for the first time ever in its long history, members arrived in such numbers that the church was literally filled. The evening service attracted another record Communion attendance. On this evidence the Kirk Session and myself sensed that our corporate labours had been blessed. But then sometimes after sunshine, there comes the gloom. At what, for me, was to prove a most unhappy Deacons' Court meeting, we were reviewing the financial position of our kirk and all the reporting was positive and encouraging because the congregation had continued to show great generosity. We had made generous provision for the support of the Mission and Service Fund throughout my ministry, and my commitment to it was in no doubt. A senior elder, who was another South Church stalwart of the old school, addressed the court. He had been an elder for many a long year; he was an evergreen in the choir for which he had great love. He was a God-fearing man and he was much respected. He was though, I regret to say, very much South Church-orientated and outreach was not his favoured course. In the event, as he spoke, he introduced a sour note into our deliberations with a diatribe directed against the National Church always looking for money. He judged, he said, that we gave much more to the Church than was necessary and he hoped an end would be made of our giving even more. He went on to suggest that this year we should halve what we gave last year. In all this I was not surprised. The speaker's view was one that met with approval from among a number of long-term office bearers who had been brought up in the congregation but who now sensed that control had passed from them. His position could be seen as a cry from the wilderness, and I hoped it would be swiftly dealt with in a considerate but firm manner. Our congregational life, after all, had been revitalised and the Deacons' Court was not made up of men acting as dinosaurs. This was a seminal moment and I knew it. Perhaps through respect for the speaker there was no rush to defend our position of providing generous support through the fund. Nobody expressed horror at our turning our backs on a world of need and I was forced to defend the past position we had taken. Indeed I was reminded of my clash with my fellow deacons four years previously when generosity towards others was not a code they easily embraced. Could all the work of the past years have been a mirage with, underneath, nothing really changed? For some, I sensed, this would be so. For the great majority though, there was much more capacity, much more intelligence and much more spiritual insight. Why had they remained silent? That was the thought I took with me as I closed the meeting. I had great respect for my office bearers but, as I reflected on the work and the witness upon which we were engaged, I slowly concluded that perhaps they viewed my aspirations as too unattainable. Did they feel that I asked and expected too much of them and possibly of our people? Could it be a case of so far and no further? In this consideration I disregarded all those whose limitations would reasonably lead to opposition. I had been dealing with such men over the past four years and more. Their opposition was to be expected and dealt with! Anyway, their silence spoke eloquently to me and I concluded that whilst I would lead I would not coerce and that, as a consequence, my usefulness to my people in Penicuik South Church had been taken as far forward as was prudent and practicable. I had been powerfully called and now, I concluded, I was being called away.

Until the telling incident in the Deacons' Court, I had

imagined that I would lead the congregation to further challenges. I was now resolved differently. Accordingly, at a meeting of the Kirk Session on 11th December 1972, I intimated to my session that it would be my intention to demit my charge by the spring of the incoming year. This arrangement, I suggested, would give both them and my family time to organise affairs. The Kirk Session, I have to say, was aghast. If a gentle reining in of my enthusiasms was the intention, this most assuredly was not the result intended. Good men, instantly, became good men again. There was much eloquent pleading that I change my mind. I was assured that I could be confident of their unwavering support. The elder who had suggested halving our outreach support, oblivious of the part he had played in that defining moment, pleaded that I should have a change of mind. The Kirk Session suggested that I should not formalise my intention with the Presbytery at this stage. Another senior elder now entered the debate to remind me that in the power of that same Spirit to whom I so often alluded, I should defer a final decision until the spring, when I could reassess what we, as a body, had achieved under the leading of the Holy Spirit. I reiterated my determination to leave my charge but, in deference to the elder's plea, I agreed to take no new initiative myself in the interim.

One immediate outcome from the distress we were all feeling was that there was no more talk of halving our support to the Mission and Service Fund. My ministry might be at risk but needy causes both at home and abroad would continue to benefit from our collective goodwill. The Deacons' Court, in a move that did nothing to increase my sense of the Holy Spirit guiding, for the first time in all my ministry, set up a committee to look at ways and means of increasing my stipend. In discussion with the office bearer who was landed with chairing this ad hoc committee, I made it quite clear that this money matter was not an issue and one that I was disinclined to consider. He well understood my position and, no doubt, reported accordingly. Upon further reflection there was so much for which to give thanks. I had presided over a vast number of Kirk Session and Deacons' Court meetings and, as was not always the case given the disturbing reports I so often heard from amongst my fellow ministers, never once in all my time was there an acrimonious shouting match. Neither was there the merest evidence of disrespect on either side. All our deliberations had been conducted in a seemly and orderly fashion and a great deal had been accomplished. I have constantly referred to the 'men' of the Kirk Session and Deacons' Court. My ministry was well advanced before I found myself in a position to propose that ladies should be eligible for ordination as deacons. There had been a seemingly intractable prejudice against ladies serving in this capacity and the opposition invariably came from the local men who valued this restriction on women serving in their domain. When I judged the time right, I proposed the then radical step change of women deacons. I was able to sugar this bitter pill by proposing a number of lifelong South Church lady members who in my view had admirable qualities of Christian commitment and fine administrative skills also. Chris Eadie, Ella Rutherford, Joy Houps and Mary Hunt, as well as some others, were in this category and were proposed, together with newer ladies to the congregation such as Helen McRae and Aubrey Gair, who displayed equal merit. These ladies were duly ordained as deacons and conspicuously performed their new duties with diligence.

The Kirk Session proved to be much more difficult. Even amongst a number of our newer and more enlightened elders there was evidence of deeply embedded prejudice. After due and proper deliberation on the question of women elders, the session judged that there was no objection to the ordination of ladies with the proviso that such ordination should only take place when there were insufficient male candidates of equal worth available for ordination. The King Canutes in our midst hoped that such a day would be long deferred. The ordination of the first lady elders in the South Church did not take place in my time but progress, in the face of prejudice, was being made.

Penicuik South Church had been vulnerable to readjustment at the time of my arrival. It was now a vibrant outward-looking kirk that had been setting standards for so many other congregations to strive after. Our kirk was now far ahead of every other congregation of measurable size in the Presbytery in terms of per capita giving. It was now the leader by this measure rather than the laggard it had traditionally been. The percentage turnout of our people at Communion was well beyond anything being witnessed in Dalkeith Presbytery, and all this against a background of falling and drifting Church membership nationally. I believed that our formula was one which the entire Church much needed in the present climate of social ferment and change, wherein Church membership generally was being devalued and eroded. We were not, though, self-publicists and there was no external trumpeting of our virtues. I took the view that quiet, patient work and witness engineered by the power of the Holy Spirit would tell in the end.

Meantime, I had to prepare for the end of my ministry. I did not know what the new year would reveal. I was now committed to remain without planning until the spring. My concern was to leave my congregation in the best possible state of health, both spiritually and materially. The spiritual side would be nurtured through worship, prayer and service. The material side could be further promoted through the General Assembly-sponsored Stewardship Campaign. This campaign highlighted the congregation's need to focus on worship, service and giving. I commended such a campaign to my already generous people as a means of reinforcing the virtues they had at least, in part, been practising.

No objection was raised and I set about gathering a keen and committed group of office bearers and others who would train in the early months of the year before systematically visiting all our members with this new challenge. As the preparation material urged, I planned to devote four sermons on successive Sundays to explain and point up the message, ahead of the campaign's start.

Some of my people were, perhaps, persuaded that all this activity might be pointing in the direction of my remaining in their midst. Then, on 6th January 1973, came a totally unexpected intervention. I received a letter from my former bishop, the Rev. James Munn, who had long since been forced into retirement because of ill health. James Munn had been invited to take Christmas and New Year services at Croftfoot Parish Church in Glasgow and had been singularly impressed with the packed church and the good spirit pervading all. Moreover, he had been so well received that in their current vacancy they had asked if he could provide any suitable recommendations. He had given them a few, based on his wide knowledge and experience. He explained that a former assistant was very much on his mind but that he was not at liberty to pass on the name without first seeking approval. Mr Munn was well acquainted with the progress of my ministry in Penicuik but he had no reason to think that I might be contemplating a move. For one thing, I had not completed the requisite five years required of a first ministry and added to which, as he stated, he had no wish to unsettle me.

My reaction was immediate. Deep was yet again calling unto deep! If I required confirmation of the rightness of my decision to move, surely this was it. I had agreed with my fellow office bearers to take no initiative on my part for some two or three months ahead. This possible solution to my future direction was coming without my pleading and planning, and in that I was greatly taken and recognised God's leading in it. I consented to Mr Munn offering my name for consideration, and immediately I was met with a response from the Vacancy Committee of Croftfoot which indicated that I would be heard.

The first delegation of four visited on the last Sunday of January and James Munn, who was preaching at Croftfoot, was collected that night by a Mr Morrison who was a leading office bearer and Vacancy Committee member. Jack Morrison had been to Penicuik in the morning and, after passing various complimentary remarks concerning myself and my conduct of the service, he suddenly shot this question to James Munn, 'Is he bossy?' My good friend and mentor denied any such suggestion and recited my apparent virtues. However, in his letter to me describing this encounter, Mr Munn wished to alert me to this perception which, if not refuted as he had been able to do, could place me at considerable disadvantage. He further counselled that I be most careful not to give any visiting committee reason to confirm Mr Morrison's fear. Jack Morrison for his part had explained that whilst he had this reservation, this had not prevented all four recommending that others hear me again. My chances, seemingly, were still alive. As I reflected on James Munn's helpful observations I could not think what I had shared with my people, or what impression I had given, that would have merited the term 'bossy'. But then I had not met Jack Morrison at that stage and I had no means of measuring the yardstick by which he could have used such a term. A second contingent visited and reported positively, such that the entire committee soon followed and were present on the last Sunday in February when I was already committed to preach on the topic of Christian stewardship. This theme did not always, I well knew, receive universal acclaim. Even so, I was happy to be judged on a subject close to my heart and to live with the consequences. As it happened, my exposition of the subject was well received, not just by the committee as a whole but by, as I was later to hear from the man himself, Jack Morrison, who placed on record his opinion that this was the best sermon on giving that he had ever heard. My congregation, for the first time that very morning, was alerted to the presence of a visiting Vacancy Committee in its midst and was reported as being much distressed. An elder and chorister whose usual choir room had been commandeered to allow the visitors to speak with me was so ruffled as to be rude. He exclaimed that they had no need to be tempting his minister from their midst. He was terribly hurt at the thought of my leaving. The entire committee wished to meet with me at length and, through Mr Munn's good offices, his successor at Newland's South, Rev. Alwyn McFarlane made suitable accommodation available and we met and had a fruitful discussion. John Wallace, the session clerk at Croftfoot, who was to become another lifelong friend, contacted me to invite me to be their sole nominee in the vacancy. With a sense of gratitude and profound conviction that God had blessed my present ministry and was calling me to new challenges, I gladly consented. Croftfoot, a large compact parish to the south of Glasgow of over two thousand homes, all of which were either privately rented or owner occupied, was a mere two miles distant from the home of my childhood and youth in the Gorbals. By a strange quirk of irony or coincidence, Croftfoot Parish Church had been transported, about the time of my birth, from the Gorbals, where its congregation had all but disappeared, to the new parish of Croftfoot, an infinitely more desirable residence. My prospective congregation did not know that in the truest and deepest sense they were about to call one of their own. But since our Lord Himself had something withering to say on this very subject; that *'a prophet is not without honour, except in his own country and in his own house'* perhaps a veil should be drawn meantime over this subject.

It was determined that I would preach as sole nominee on Sunday 18th March 1973, when for the second time in my experience, I would preach for acceptance. I duly did so and was thereafter elected as their new minister. Croftfoot would be a challenging proposition since it had a congregation close on thirteen hundred and fifty. It was led by a numerically strong Kirk Session comprising some seventy male members, together with a large Congregational Board with both sexes represented.

The Sunday before I preached at Croftfoot, I was faced with the melancholy task of informing my Penicuik South morning congregation that it was most likely that I would soon be departing. I knew that I would find this intimation the most difficult I had ever had to make but, in truth, I underestimated the effect it had upon me. My chief difficulty lay in the array of fixed and stony faces that confronted me as I spoke. I shall never forget that moment, and in particular the look on the face of Mrs Logan, whose dear husband, the Rev. Frank Logan, I had so recently buried and who, I knew, looked to me for solace and comfort in her present extreme old age. She and Frank, a veteran of the First World War, had no children, and in their latter years had delighted to offer Rena and me, together with Douglas and Gillian, the warmest of hospitality. The congregation registered a widespread sense of something akin to bereavement and I felt pierced and guilty.

My valedictory service came at the close of a week or two of special goodbyes being said, sometimes over a meal, where we were able to reflect on the events and circumstances that had helped make secure the friendships we now shared. The congregation lavished gifts and prayerful good wishes upon us and we took our leave of them to attempt to further advance Christ's kingdom in ways which would be pleasing to God and which would not conflict with the integrity of my high calling.

After almost five years in the east of Scotland, we said farewell to Penicuik.

Chapter Eight

On Wednesday evening, 16th May, a new phase in my ministry was about to open with my Induction Service in the face of a packed congregation. Provision had been made in church for a large contingent of friends and well-wishers from Penicuik, and as the service commenced their space remained unoccupied. A stir was created in the assembled congregation with the late arrival of our Penicuik friends whose bus had had mechanical troubles on its journey from east to west. I mention this because the delay in arrival was but the precursor of a much longer delay in the return journey, which saw them reach Penicuik at one o'clock in the morning. But among the fifty or so passengers, there remained one very irrepressible old lady who maintained good humour throughout – Mrs Graham. This of course was the same old lady who eighteen months before had been all but dead. She had made good her sensing that God still had some work for her to accomplish and also, so it seemed, some social relaxation too. My finding her present at my induction made the event more memorable on that one count alone.

In the course of the social that followed on from the service, it gave me particular pleasure to have the Rev.

James Munn speak on my behalf in the elevating tones and great spiritual verve that were so characteristic of him and of his generation of fine Scottish churchmen. My close friend and contemporary, the Rev. Sandy McDonald, spoke very expressively with the wit and humour that was music to my Glasgow-based audience's ears. All in all, the entire evening provided a most promising backcloth to the hard work that was in prospect.

James Munn, in one of his regular letters to me, in the run up to my induction, had spoken of how he had viewed his earlier call to his main work in the Church, as a knowledgeable minister, as rather akin to an experience of forgiveness. In this, he was asserting that after the years and experiences of a first ministry, now much matured, he could jettison that which had not worked and concentrate on that which had been successful. The observation was valid. Penicuik South had offered a blueprint of the possible and, on the much larger canvas of Croftfoot, I would have the opportunity to drive forward my vision of a congregation of God's people hurtling into the fray and setting standards of witness and service not previously considered. The likelihood would be that, in tune with Mr Munn's thoughts, my present congregation would be the main theatre of my life's work in the ministry.

The fellowship I inherited was a strong worshipping one, not to be wondered at given the size of the congregation. The measure that was most telling was that over the past number of years, in the course of a Communion Sunday involving three diets of worship, almost exactly fifty per cent of the congregation attended. Much closer pastoral oversight, I knew, could greatly improve the present response. Financially, the congregation was clearly outward-looking. At the time of my arrival, it was offering 3.3 times the amount that Penicuik South had attained in the support of the Mission and Service Fund of the National Church. In Penicuik and throughout Dalkeith Presbytery, our response to the support of this fund was seen as extraordinary. In Croftfoot, the elders and office bearers took their much vaster support of the fund in their stride and totally without complaint. They were responding to that which had been asked of them, and this attitude, I have to say, I found entirely honouring. Even so, I also understood that I had been called to lead my new people in this particular part of God's vineyard and I did not doubt that there still lay hidden untapped resources available to the kirk.

I quickly learned from the session clerk and other leading office bearers that their view was that my predecessor, the Rev. James McNay, had been a very acceptable and gifted preacher but that his pastoral work had been very weak. He had no appetite at all for general visiting and, indeed, made quite a point of advising prospective new members that his present meeting with them would be his last. They, on the other hand, could see him every Sunday. James McNay had a reputation for brusqueness and it was quite evident why this was so! In this latter sense he was not going to prove a hard act to follow.

It was against this general information that I found myself with my first regular meeting, which happened not to be with the Kirk Session but with the Congregational Board. The previous minister had elected not to be chairman of the board and had delegated this important function to another board member, Mr Bill Kerr. It was not my wish to be excluded from the chairmanship and I made this immediately clear, to avoid speculation or confusion. I was also sensitive to the 'new broom' syndrome that could bring with it one or two little problems. Bill Kerr well understood my prerogative in this matter and graciously assented. One or two others on the board hierarchy had, I sensed, a feeling that things would not be quite the same. After all, their previous man had not interfered!

I constituted my first meeting, offered one or two introductory remarks and then got down to the business agenda. I invited the first report, the all-important treasurer's report, and the church treasurer provided this. I was immediately aware, in the manner of his reporting and the content of the report, that the treasurer was making a special point that had to do with his providing information on his terms. The report was entirely uninformative and, when he had concluded, I knew I had to respond and do so decisively. I turned to him and thanked him for his 'somewhat cursory report', sensing that this young man was going to provide some sort of running sore. I need not have worried. He looked at me, stood up and, in a fury, threw down his pen, declared himself resigned and intimated that he would not remain a moment longer – and he did not. Off he went, leaving the meeting flabbergasted. So here was I, barely minutes into my first meeting and I had lost my congregational treasurer.

Where, I wondered, was the great goodwill with which I had been received into the bosom of the congregation just days before? I was just about to assure the Congregational Board that I had no great track record at losing treasurers in this manner when it became clear that the board were themselves both disturbed at this dislocation and sympathetic towards their new minister who had been confronted by this strange spectacle. Almost instantly, the lady who had been assisting the treasurer indicated that if the board so pleased she would immediately undertake the duties of treasurer pro tem. The board heaved a collective sigh of relief and Mrs Pearl Smith was appointed there and then. Pearl Smith, both in name and in nature, was to become a very good friend and was to prove an invaluable asset to Croftfoot Church throughout my entire ministry there.

Working in tandem with myself in the guiding of the material wellbeing of the congregation was the clerk to the board, Mrs Margaret Williamson, who was another of those treasures that the Church regularly reveals, in that she was a lifelong member, totally dedicated to serving and helping forward the cause of Christ from where she was rooted.

The session clerk, John Wallace, was an absolute stalwart

within the leadership of the congregation. John possessed the virtue of cheerfulness in abundance. Apart from that he was transparently honest and honourable. He was employed by British Railways in administration at management level and, in Church matters, was a superlative administrator. If John had any fault at all, and who amongst us is without, it was that he could think ill of no one; he did not always discern between the good and the not so good. His faith was not a matter for display but was securely and deeply held and he certainly lived up to it. His wife and soul mate, Barbara, was a Yorkshire girl whom he had met during his wartime service and to whom he was totally devoted. A common thread connecting John and myself was that we had both in our early lives been sergeants in the army and, moreover, we had both been in the Cameron Highlanders. John offered me undisguised and enduring friendship and was foursquare behind my spiritual and temporal leadership from day one of my ministry right through to its completion. The minister, session clerk, clerk to the Congregational Board and treasurer were as one in our endeavours on behalf of our people in both congregation and parish. We hoped that by working together in a caring way, Croftfoot would present a seemly and compelling witness. I was aware, from the very beginning at Croftfoot, of the marked contrast between the two communities of Penicuik and Croftfoot. There was a large range of intellectual and spiritual capability in the much smaller of the two congregations. In Penicuik, my Kirk Session had been drawn from a wide range of men with very diverse backgrounds. One of our much-loved elders was a street cleaner and a finer man it would be difficult to meet. At the other end of the spectrum we shared office with senior executives, businessmen of experience and, in one instance, with an army colonel who, again, was a most charming and committed Christian man. These men, given the diverse experience that they had, both within and without the Church, well understood the issues we had engaged in at Penicuik South Church. Not all agreed but they did understand the issues.

Croftfoot, on the other hand, was a single layer community, in the very nature of which, and given its roots, was essentially comprised of well-doing, upright, ordinary folk. It possessed virtually no professional people. Those in the midst who had shown most promise had all moved on. Its large Kirk Session and Congregational Board had but a sprinkling of progressive able-thinking people. I could also see that it would never be possible to recruit people of such talent into the congregation given the closed nature of the community. If Croftfoot were ever to make a distinctive witness beyond its boundaries then it would have to be the case of ordinary people achieving extraordinary results. The question for me at the outset was – could they be so led? I judged that they could!

I had emphasised the virtues of Christian stewardship to my people in Penicuik and I had strongly led them along that route to the point when I understood that they needed a change of leader to confirm and consolidate the ground we had won. I would now engage my new-found people in a witness involving the thoughtful providing of their time, their talents and their money. The starting point for this entire endeavour had been for their new minister first of all to win their confidence and consequently their support. I immediately endeavoured to discover the extent of the elderly and their whereabouts. This presented no problem at all. John Wallace, I found, was a great 'list' man. Soon, armed with copious background information, I set about systematic visitation of the infirm and the very elderly, of whom Croftfoot had no shortage. I have recorded elsewhere my appreciation of the influence of the Boys' Brigade upon my childhood development. Here in Croftfoot, I now found myself the minister of Miss Bessie Nelson, who had been the pianist of our Life Boy Team within the 73rd BB Company. This lady, and she was a very nice lady, had accompanied at the piano one night when Diana Tibbert had gently withdrawn me from the choir because of my choral limitations. Bessie Nelson had looked on sympathetically at the wee boy's banishment. Now not only was Miss Nelson a loyal member of our congregation but her continuing friendship with Diana Tibbert resulted in Diana now quite regularly worshipping with us at our evening service after having faithfully attended her own church in the morning. Diana Tibbert, I should also mention, had remained a dear friend who corresponded with me throughout my army career and was also a guest at our wedding. She had lived to witness the young lad whom she, on first meeting, had called 'Sonny' become her best friend's minister. Another similar role change of some note was that my former technical subjects teacher at Strathbungo School, Mr Matt Kincaid, was also a member of my congregation, and since his wife Millie was a semi-invalid I had occasion to visit with some frequency and so ministered to one who had earlier taught me.

These special situations apart, my recurring elderly visitation and my assiduous attention to hospital visitation were in tune with the best hopes of the congregation at large. In another and less expected way, there was a strengthening of bonds. Croftfoot by the 1970s was an ageing congregation, if for no other reason than that the youngish families who came into the new communities of the 1930s were now in their old age. Consequently, there was a steady increase in the number of deaths among members. On the understanding of there being opportunity in extremity, I was now regularly making contact with families in bereavement. These sometimes distressing and often perplexing situations provided ample opportunity for pastoral counsel and for the formation of new relationships of mutuality and regard. My conviction and experience that close caring pastoral oversight was the key to congregational health was being put to the test. My ministry progressed along these lines for the first year or thereby.

I had taken careful note of the congregation's financial

strength since my arrival earlier in the year and had noted that during the vacancy there had been a measurable if not large drop in financial support. By the year's end this drop had been reversed and a modest gain made. The schemes of the church, our expression of our support for maintenance of ministry and mission and service agencies, asked for and received sums amounting to thirty-seven per cent of the total congregational income. I had certainly not inherited the spirit of introspection which had so marked my introduction to Penicuik South. Our much more ordinary people in Croftfoot had an infinitely better and more generous approach to the issue of helping others. The challenge before me would not be one of winning support for the notion of helping others but would rather be one of fanning up and inflaming support for the work of Christ beyond our doors.

The folk who made up my large congregation made no special claim as to their spirituality. Unlike my previous congregation, we had no element of lively born-again Christians with conservative evangelical conviction; no thwarted Baptists (Penicuik had no Baptist Church) who felt they had to 'make do' with the Church of Scotland. There was a Baptist Church available nearby. If the Croftfoot congregation was to make any claim, it would be that it aspired to practical Christianity.

This position was displayed in different ways. The folk in Croftfoot rejoiced in local fundraising. The Christmas fayre was the centrepiece of vigorous and productive fund-raising. The convener of the fabric committee, Mr John Habbick, linked up with John Wallace in organising this astonishing annual event, which saw the Church's ample hall suite, comprising five different-sized areas, being simply flooded with many hundreds of local people. The Christmas fayre was a Croftfoot Church institution that employed huge resources but which, on the day of the event, raised a very large amount of money within two hours. Almost rivalling this enterprise was the annual jumble sale. This required vast amounts of behind the scenes activity but which, in its turn, raised such a large sum that almost any other church would have been proud to claim its outcome as their major fund-raising enterprise. This was not so in Croftfoot, where this event was always understood as very subsidiary.

When I arrived, another fundraising venture, exclusively controlled and run by the menfolk, with Mr Jack Morrison very much in charge, was the collection and sale of waste paper. This exercise was carried out like a mini industry and, at the time, raised very considerable sums for church funds. It was very clear that the men and women of Croftfoot knew quite a lot about giving of their time and talents to help forward the cause of the church.

By the beginning of 1974, I reckoned that sufficient groundwork had been accomplished to allow minister and office bearers to meet together in conference and plan a stratagem for strengthening our church finances. This conference was warmly agreed to and scheduled for 12.30 p.m. following morning worship on February 3rd 1974.

It was arranged that, before the meeting, we would share a meal together in fellowship as a prelude to the formal business. Our first session dealt with the present standard of membership. Was it satisfactory? Who should give a lead in an effort towards improvement? Was Communion attendance a sufficient test of membership? Session two dealt with temporal matters related to giving. How could we as leaders set an example to the rest of the congregation? What was our attitude to giving towards purposes highlighted by the church? How could we alert sleeping members to the needs of the church? Did we consider that offerings should be sacrificial?

All these questions led to full and often animated discussion, and I discerned evidence of a new awareness developing on the issues raised. Covenanted giving was well aired and it was largely agreed that we, as office bearers, should be in the vanguard of our promoting this scheme that was so obviously tax-effective and, of course, beneficial to the church.

The conference had been stimulating and I was confident that we would soon witness fresh shoots of growth. New impetus was given to the levels of our weekly offerings and the congregation began to see evidence of increases from the monthly magazine reports such as had not been seen before. I was being confirmed in my view that when the office bearers embraced a new generosity they would be properly equipped to offer guidance to the members within their care.

By the summer, I was reporting in our church magazine, along the lines to which I have alluded, that we had been a much-bereaved fellowship in the course of the past year. I intimated that I had buried no fewer than fifty of our members or parishioners during the past twelve months. Because of the demography of our parish, we could not be other than a very depleted congregation in the years to come. I offered a clarion call to all our people that our lives should be lived worthily and in keeping with the inspiration of Jesus' own life and of those whom we had loved and whose memories we would forever cherish.

Towards the end of the year, the Congregational Board met to consider our financial situation and how we should respond to the claims made upon us as stewards of our resources. Ahead of our meeting, I had found myself in conversation with the Rev. Tom McFarlane, minister of South Shawlands Church. Tom was a leading member of the Glasgow Presbytery Stewardship and Budget Committee and also of the General Assembly Committee. There were over two hundred churches in the Presbytery, and it was his responsibility to scrutinise them all. He thought to have an encouraging word with me. 'Hugh,' he said, 'your congregation is bearing an inordinate burden in terms of its Mission and Service allocation. I think I can promise that we will set a lower and less burdensome figure for next year!' I assured him immediately that I wished no relaxation whatsoever in our allocation. Our people found the large sum required more of a challenge than a burden. Tom McFarlane looked slightly perplexed but he understood what I was saying.

When our Congregational Board meeting was convened, the treasurer was able to report a twenty-eight per cent increase in the year's liberality. Such a gain in a single year could never have been contemplated by any of our office bearers throughout their entire time in office, and much gratitude was expressed over this wonderful movement forward. Most happy of all, so far as I was concerned, was the expressed willingness to offer much in excess of our allocation to the Mission and Service Fund. The allocation, as it was, represented the highest figure we had ever been called upon to make (hence Tom McFarlane's anxiety on our behalf) but even so, we added a further twenty-nine per cent beyond what was invited. By this gracious act, Croftfoot had taken a first step towards a witness and an example to the whole Church. This was an exemplary act and one that I trusted would be progressive.

The work of the New Year had barely begun and I became aware that the good resolutions associated with the season are soon forgotten. I was concerned that there be no relaxation of our endeavours, and I was looking forward very much to the joint conference of elders and board members to prepare the ground for our stewardship outreach to the entire congregation. Towards this end, I wrote early in January to the congregation, outlining the background to the Church of Scotland 'Give As You Earn' campaign, which the Presbytery was pressing that every congregation should embrace. In my letter, I explained that the scheme would become effective as from Sunday 16th April 1975 and ahead of this starting date I would preach on the theme of Christian stewardship on the three preceding Sundays. The conference, held on Sunday 15th February, preceded by a bonding lunch, was addressed by Mr Will Farrell on behalf of the General Assembly Stewardship and Budget Committee, and he spoke very effectively and persuasively. The final piece in the jigsaw, so far as preparation was concerned, was the securing of a strong and committed team from amongst our Kirk Session and board members. Margaret Williamson, who was already proving to be a most able and efficient clerk to the board, drafted a challenging letter in the hope and expectation of a concerted response from our office bearers. The response from the board was magnificent and Margaret had little difficulty in arranging teams for visitation.

Just days before this communication was directed to those in office, the Annual Stated Meeting had taken place on Monday 10th March. The meeting agreed to changes in our board constitution to enable the elected members to be increased from twenty-four to thirty, with a similar new number of thirty being appointed from the Kirk

Session. Thus the newly expanded board of sixty was even better placed to oversee the material affairs of our new vibrant congregation. With the visitation successfully completed and the programme of 'Give As You Earn' implemented at the beginning of April, I was able to report on the phenomenal success of the scheme by as early as the May edition of our magazine, *Gleanings*.

On Sundays 2nd and 9th March, when I preached on the theme of giving, ahead of the scheme implementation, the congregational offerings over these two Sundays increased by an unprecedented sixty-one per cent. We were witnessing a totally new level of giving and our outreach was being blessed in an astonishing way. My hope was that we would remain worthy stewards of our increasing resources.

News of the happenings at Croftfoot was filtering down to Presbytery level and the good people of Croftfoot were beginning to be seen in a new light. As I met with friends and colleagues at Presbytery, I was prepared to commend the generosity of my people and I thought I took great care to avoid the merest hint of triumphalism, of which I had an innate distaste. Even so, the Church was in some considerable financial difficulty and if our approach and method could contribute to the greater wellbeing of all, then this had to be good. Action, I was convinced, would speak more eloquently than words!

Chapter Nine

We had made wonderful progress financially. I was keener still to see evidence of further strengthening on other fronts. I had initiated a systematic scheme of congregational visitation, and I had placed on record my intention to seek no respite until I had accomplished this formidable task. Our congregation consisted of fifty-four elders' districts, and being aware of the defective psychology of starting at district one and hoping to wade through to the last, leading to deferred expectation, I opted for a different route. I placed all fifty-four numbers in a hat and drew them out in the order that I would visit. My next resort was to intimate the actual district number on the Sunday ahead of my proposed visitation. By so devising, I kept afloat a high level of expectation and, no doubt, in some few cases, of apprehension.

The year was notable too in that we achieved what had never been possible with my previous congregation. Before our usual well-packed church I was privileged to ordain the first lady elders to office in Croftfoot. Six ladies who had mostly served with distinction on the Congregational Board were encouraged to overcome their historic reserve and were duly admitted to office. The Kirk Session by this time had been mobilised to take heed of members who had no appetite or inclination for worship. The supplementary roll was reconstituted and good use was now being made of it. We were consciously honing our roll well, realising that mere names on the roll in no way added to the vitality of the church. Many of our elders had been quickened to a new awareness of their functions and had been diligently seeking to enthuse their district members. The fruits of their collective efforts were soon evident. Writing in our October edition of *Gleanings,* I was able to express my personal thanks and appreciation for the phenomenon we had witnessed on Communion Sunday, 14th September, when we gathered in numbers not seen in Croftfoot Church for many years, and this against a backdrop of our now being an appreciably smaller (however, numerically still large) congregation than in years past. We continued to be blessed in so many areas of our service. I intimated at this time the formation of our Adult Christian Education Group that would now meet regularly in the interest of office bearers and members alike. This forum, I explained, would offer an environment for serious, mature Christian study for any who felt insecure or uncertain, or for those who sensed that they might have knowledge and experience in the faith, which they were prepared to share.

At the end of the year, Pearl Smith, our treasurer, was at hand to report that congregational income had leapt yet again in dramatic fashion by a staggering forty-eight per cent beyond last year's vast increase. The Congregational

Board had no hesitation in looking to enhance our required Mission and Service Fund allocation and provided fifty-nine per cent more than requested. At the same meeting, a considerable sum was voted towards a Local Churches' Appeal to assist our struggling neighbouring church, Castlemilk East, in a move to help them pay off a disabling standing debt on their church building. I was soon in receipt of a most kind acknowledgement from the minister, the Rev. John Miller, expressing particular appreciation for the thoughtfulness and generosity of our people at Croftfoot. We were fast becoming a force for good in a continuing needy Church. My people were doing well in an area where their capabilities and temperament had fitted them so to do, and I took pride in their accomplishment.

On the domestic front, we had all now been long settled into our manse at Viewpark Drive in Burnside. Douglas and Gillian were both pupils at the local school, Stonelaw High, and were performing very well indeed. Our family had been added to by the addition of a stray dog Douglas had picked up during the rounds of his part-time job. Sandy was a mongrel of about a year when rescued, and he remained a great favourite with us throughout his long lifes and we grieved when he died.

We were living through an inflationary spiral and we were without a home of our own since the sale of our previous house in Cathcart in 1969. It now seemed prudent that I make some provision for the security of our family in terms of housing. Toward this end we bought a flat in Largs and this would also serve the purpose of providing holiday accommodation for us during my summer break. We also had, in this manner, regained a foothold in the property market and secured a hedge against inflation. Rena had also obtained a part-time appointment within the Pharmaceutical Society as their pharmacy drug-testing inspector covering central Scotland. She was to prove a very popular inspector indeed with her gentle and friendly approach. This same approach she had ever employed with dealing with our church family where, again, she was hugely popular and an undoubted asset to my ministry.

By this time also, I had been identified by my colleagues in Presbytery as a suitable leader of the Presbytery Stewardship and Budget Committee, and I was appointed convener. Many of the congregations within Presbytery had struggled to meet the needs of the wider Church and a good number had signally failed to meet the challenge. In a measured and thoughtful way, I believed I could be of service to the Presbytery in this matter and I relished the prospect. I had ever been convinced that leadership should always be from the front and, to be effective, the leader's credentials should stand up to scrutiny. My people in Croftfoot had provided the outer credibility by their stewardship. My inner credibility belonged to my personal and totally private commitment to a cause, which I knew to be truly worthy. I set the Presbytery committee to the task of clearly identifying congregations that were struggling badly and also those that, by any yardstick, were performing poorly. The list eventually was large. We knew that systematic visitation and encouragement would take considerable time, and not a little patience, if we were to make an impression. But try we would!

Within my congregation we worked at consolidating the gains of the last year and as the year progressed we observed continued growth. Our gathered Sunday congregations continued to provide encouragement, and I strove to retain freshness and diversity in public worship by resorting to a policy whereby I invited a guest preacher of some eminence to conduct Sunday services from time to time. I had not sought to engage an assistant, as most other large congregations like ours did, simply because I wished to remain totally focussed on leading my people to new and challenging objectives. Training or guiding an assistant was not a present priority. The introduction of a distinguished preacher, on the other hand, would edify and also provide me with occasional Sunday relaxation. The Kirk Session concurred, and I was able to introduce a fair number of my former professors and lecturers from Trinity College and they were received with much enthusiasm.

As the year progressed it was beginning to dawn on a number of our office bearers that we in Croftfoot were now a 'rich' church, and that money should be made available more freely for internal use. This was, of course, a variation of the theme that charity begins at home. An interesting feature of this emerging doctrine was that it was chiefly embraced by folk who had no enthusiasm for Christian stewardship and especially if it threatened their own pocket. This was a development which, although deeply disappointing, was one that in no way surprised me since I had experienced a similar phenomenon at Penicuik South. I was identifying an arena for potential conflict. At board level, the finance committee, recognising these dissident stirrings, was guided to propose to the entire Congregational Board that in the event of further financial strengthening of congregational resources, we should allocate fifty per cent of this additional revenue for internal purposes and fifty per cent to the work of the wider Church. I hoped that this stratagem would ensure that our focus would not become introspective and self-defeating. We were not, after all, a business seeking to make a profit to satisfy our shareholders.

In December, our ebullient treasurer reported that our income had advanced by a further twelve and a half per cent and, issuing from this, it was proposed, with internal funds prospering, that we contribute an additional eighty per cent above our requested Mission and Service Fund allocation. The board received this proposal with acclamation and I was proud yet again of the selflessness of my people. It was a good note on which to end 1976.

The incoming year presented the usual challenges and the Kirk Session and Congregational Board remained impressively active. The elders observed diligent pre-

Communion visitation and reported back to the session. The board members carried out their now annual 'Give As You Earn' calls on their people. I was ever more involved at Presbytery level and found myself much engaged in committee work, not just with the Stewardship and Budget Committee, but also with the Maintenance of the Ministry Committee where there was an overlap of interest and responsibility. I was also now required to represent Glasgow Presbytery on the General Assembly Stewardship and Budget Committee and from that vantage point I was gaining new insights into the workings of the Church establishment at 121 George Street, Edinburgh.

By 1977, it was now widely understood that the Church of Scotland was facing a financial crisis. The national press carried sometimes lurid stories as to the extent of the crisis and its likely effects upon the work of the Church if it were not arrested and reversed. The Very Rev. Andrew Herron, writing in an article headed 'Kirk Feels Cash Pinch' on 17th February 1977, chastised unthinking Church members saying, 'One should give according to one's means, not according to one's meanness'. At Croftfoot, we were in the vanguard of the movement seeking review and recommitment amongst our people, with our conference on such matters scheduled for 20th February. Inflation was continuing to devastate the value of the country's charitable giving and an awareness of this had to be driven home.

Congregational life throughout 1977 was extremely active

and rewarding and I felt engaged and fulfilled. In the late summer I had arranged, among others, for a recently retired minister within the Presbytery to conduct our services. He duly did so and he was much taken by our large, friendly and attentive congregation. So much so that I soon received a letter from him enquiring about the possibility of his attaching himself to Croftfoot Church as my assistant. He went further; he outlined the financial terms on which he would be happy to serve should I be interested in making use of his services. This retired minister was a man who had a very good reputation in the Church, and his earlier ministry in the war years and after, in the Presbytery of Glasgow, was remembered with great affection. He had created a club and a centre for young people that had an enduring impact and which had achieved much social gain in a deprived area. He had been a good friend of my dear mentor, James Munn, within whose company I had first met him. I had been greatly taken by his combination of high seriousness and compelling sense of humour.

I had to think long and hard about his offer. He would have firm views on a whole range of issues and the question of compatibility could arise. I needed answers to these questions, not directly so, but gained through a thorough discussion with him as to our respective roles. I responded to his letter and we met and discussed the possibility of our working together. He acknowledged possible pitfalls but assured me that he was entirely happy in the supporting role into which he was offering himself.

He would be completely under my direction and, as he expressed it, his regard for my ministry and me was such that he was confident of a happy collaboration. I was equally impressed by his openness and his insights into possible difficulties, given a mismatch of personality and the like. I duly took his offer to my Kirk Session, and the membership was happy to concur to our personal arrangement, and so it was that by October 1977 I had a acquired a most able assistant. From the very outset we agreed that our names would appear jointly in relation to the conduct of public worship, and I would naturally determine his participation. As a rule of thumb, the assistant would lead and preach at worship in the ratio of one service to four. In this manner we set forth to further serve our people and to strengthen them in their faith.

Our adjusted ministry was well received and my new assistant's sermons found much acceptance amongst our congregation. For my own part, I found that his sermons exhibited the distillation of much experience, but there was, to my understanding, a gloomy aspect to them that slightly jarred. My assistant also participated in my scheme of ongoing visitation of the elderly within the congregation, and his undoubted pastoral gifts and sensitivity when encountering our elderly proved most popular. Rena, herself, when in hospital, was visited by my assistant and she also found him to be a helpful and comforting hospital visitor.

Another year reached its climax and, at our December

Congregational Board meeting, the board was pleased to ratify our recommendation from the finance committee that our Mission and Service allocation be exceeded by a further eighty per cent. This extra, they judged, was completely affordable in a year which had seen our congregational income increase by sixteen per cent.

As we advanced into 1978 the General Treasurer of the Church of Scotland, W.G.P. Colledge, wrote to our congregational treasurer in these terms, 'The substantial excess beyond allocation by your congregation to the Mission and Service Fund is to be greatly admired and applauded. On behalf of the Church I send you its sincere gratitude and appreciation.' George Elliot, secretary of the Assembly's Stewardship and Budget Committee, wrote in similar vein, as did the secretaries of the Home Board and the Overseas Council.

Whilst our financial affairs in Croftfoot had never ever been stronger, the opposite was the case with regard to the Church of Scotland as a whole, and the word 'crisis' was now being bandied about with good reason. On the back of a General Assembly Committee initiative, I addressed our congregation on this issue on Sunday 26th February 1978, preparatory to our office bearers visiting our people to initiate pledges of support to the ongoing 'Give As You Earn' scheme. There were now distinct rumblings of dissent amongst a small coterie of men and women who held office but who in my view did not adorn it. They had mainly been long-time office bearers who, whilst not in tune with the present thrust of leadership, were, even so, determined to hang on to their office come what may. It may be discerned from these observations that I was now quite persuaded that within the leadership of our congregation, there were reactionary forces that would not easily be displaced. The work proceeded not because of them, but rather in spite of them.

An item of business came before the Kirk Session that was to prove divisive. Our church officer was attaining retirement age and we had to reach a decision on his future. A committee was duly formed and considered all the issues. Large congregations in the Church of Scotland had a tradition of full-time church officers who were frequently housed by the congregation, or their accommodation paid for, if not owned, by the Church. Full-time church officers were now under threat, as many congregations could not now afford to provide them. Our committee investigated the workload of the church officer and whether, in as objectively as possible a manner, he could be said to be fully employed. The committee concluded that if it were considering an appointment with, as it were, a blank sheet, then a part-time appointment would be appropriate. Adjustments would have to be made in terms of service and part-time cleaners would be appointed. Given that our church officer was due to retire and that we were responsible for providing his rented accommodation, the committee concluded that we should offer him continued employment on a part-time basis with the proviso that we employed cleaners to take over that area of his former responsibility. We would of course continue to provide his accommodation. This was understood to be forward planning in the best interests of the congregation and linked to a responsible use of resources in terms of stewardship.

It emerged that the church officer was not too pleased with the outcome, although he had not expressed this position in his interview with the committee members who had met with him to outline their proposals. A small number of elders, folk in some cases close to and friendly with the church officer, and in some cases people who thought that stewardship in Croftfoot had gone far enough, reacted and expressed their views at the session meeting when the matter was under discussion. Now this was all very proper and all views required to be heard. What was not proper, and not at all expected, now occurred. My assistant, who was present at the Kirk Session as an act of courtesy and not as a member and therefore not entitled to speak, rose to his feet and proceeded to address the session. He was clearly agitated and began to forcefully plead the case for the need of a congregation like Croftfoot, with all its resources, to maintain a full-time church officer. I allowed him to proceed no further. I rose and reminded him politely but firmly that surely he knew that he had no right to address the court at all and would he please resume his seat.

This of course was a defining moment. I was horrified at my assistant's intervention. It betokened all manner of problems for our mutuality into the future. I was well aware that he, together with his wife, had developed a good friendship with our church officer. The latter was, in turn, an admirer of my assistant, if simply respectful of me. Moreover, my assistant was a devoted and, it could fairly be said, a fanatical supporter of Glasgow Rangers Football Club and, in that, at Croftfoot, he was not alone. He had made common cause with one or two of my fellow elders whom I had reason to keep at a slight distance based on their seemingly blind allegiance to a football team, which surpassed all their other interests. I, as it were, had been brought up on the slopes of Ibrox since my childhood, but I retained a sense of proportion when it came to making a religion of this attachment.

The Kirk Session continued its discussion, with my assistant sitting head bowed, deep in thought, and went on to approve the committee's report and to implement the post of part-time church officer from the date of our church officer's retirement age. I knew that the harmony that had been the mark of my ministry at Croftfoot had been disturbed and that it would never be restored. Was this, I wondered, the price of so-called success? There always had to be a price.

By the time my assistant and I next had occasion to meet, we had both had time to think carefully about the unhappy incident that had occurred. He clearly did not deem it a resigning matter, though had I been in his place I would have thought it might have merited that conclusion. For my part, to call for his resignation would have added to the distress already occasioned. On balance, to forgive and attempt to forget appeared the only policy. Consequently, we both departed from the unhappy matter.

In the course of 1978, a regalvanised Presbytery Stewardship and Budget Committee had continued to visit struggling congregations within the bounds and I personally was much involved in providing a lead here by choosing on behalf of my committee to meet and engage with the most entrenched and failing of our congregations. Our corporate efforts had delivered good Presbytery performance up to the end of 1977 and there was now evidence to be confident that Glasgow Presbytery, the largest Presbytery by far in the Church of Scotland, was going to do better than for some considerable time in its collective response to the needs of the Church.

Nearer the end of the year, I was confronted by another most unhappy development. The church choir had within its ranks a number of members who were also office bearers and who were displaying evidence of disaffection. Church choirs often have their own agendas and sometimes have to be nursed and regularly praised. Our organist, who was a very serious-minded and gifted choirmaster, led our choir. He well understood that I neither professed nor indeed possessed any measurable musical qualities, save a willingness to participate with enthusiasm in our congregational singing. However, as with all church organists, he was under the direction and control of the minister in the conduct of public worship. This was a reality throughout the Church of Scotland and, depending on the temperament of the organist, it could sometimes rankle.

Whatever was the background, Pearl Smith, our treasurer, had to report to the finance committee that the choir had incurred some small expense and now sought repayment. Unfortunately they had not obtained approval of the Congregational Board in the acknowledged way. The sum involved was small, but the ignoring of the board was viewed by some, including myself, as a statement of disregard for the board's procedures in these matters. If the choir could have resort to congregational funds without authority, could not others? This would not do. The choir would have to be challenged and the situation regularised. No one doubted that this small sum should have been forthcoming, but the choir would need to observe rules that existed to protect all congregational funds from being used without authority. I knew the matter to be delicate and I was suspicious as to its origins, and I also felt that our treasurer should be spared the discomfort of having to raise the matter with our organist. I spoke to him at the conclusion of our morning Christmas Family Service and he instantly claimed that this small sum was as nothing to a church such as ours and in a mood of extreme anger he threatened to resign on the spot and also to refuse to conduct the service due that evening which, as it happened, was a Choir Praise Service. I urged him to calm down and reconsider his position. He moved towards the door, seething and white with anger, and I quickly placed myself between him and the door. It did not seem to me that our interview should end in this abrupt and alarming manner. He momentarily suggested that I was improperly detaining him. I retorted that my concern was that this matter required to be resolved now. If he were determined to resign then that should happen, but our service that night required his attendance, as did the choir. He had by now composed himself and indicated that for the choir's sake he would involve himself that evening but that his resignation would be forthcoming. My feeling was that his resignation would be appropriate. This was proving to be a most eventful year and one from which I was deriving no pleasure.

Even so, internal machinations apart, our congregational life had never been more buoyant, with over eighty-six per cent of the entire congregation appearing at least once in the year at Communion. This was a figure almost beyond comprehension for the Church of Scotland, and especially so when consideration was given to the large number of aged and infirm in our midst for whom church attendance was no longer a possibility. Our people were witnessing a good confession and on that count they were much to be honoured. Pearl Smith brought to the board the information that receipts for the year had amounted to £38,350 (in today's value £230,000), an increase of thirty per cent over receipts for 1977. The recommendation was proposed that the Mission and Service Fund receive forty-four per cent extra beyond the record high allocation now set by Presbytery, based on our vastly higher income than hitherto. Upon interpretation, this meant that in 1978 Croftfoot provided Mission and Service Fund support as follows:

Allocation 1978 £6,100 (today's value £37,000)
Total given 1978 £8,800 (today's value £53,000)

It is clear from these figures the extent of the congregation's generosity at the time and why it was judged by the church to have made a conspicuous effort in showing the way forward for others. Croftfoot was a congregation with a very modest income level. The many surrounding suburban congregations had a much higher income profile and in almost every case could not compare with Croftfoot's response. In my role as Presbytery Convener I had been much empowered by my own congregation as I exhorted over two hundred other kirks to strive after more thoughtful giving. The clarion call that 'it is more blessed to give than to receive' was being sounded and, early in 1979, I addressed Presbytery with the information that congregations within the bounds had supported the Mission and Service outreach as never before.

Chapter Ten

I was now well into my sixth year of ministry at Croftfoot and I sensed dark clouds gathering. The Congregational Board had been alerted by the Presbytery's Maintenance of the Ministry Committee as to a new stipend structure, which was to become effective from 1st January 1979. This communication had been received by the board late in 1978 and it was offered for information only since it was the Presbytery committee's prerogative, under instruction from the General Assembly's committee, to set stipend levels. The bombshell, so far as some of our board members were concerned, was that my stipend was set to increase from £3,440.00 per annum to £5,337.00 – a massive increase of fifty-five per cent. The background to this increase was that there had been no reappraisal of stipends generally for a good many years. The Maintenance of the Ministry Committee insisted that the appropriate rate for a congregation of our standing was the rate they were now implementing. The stipend, they insisted, was paid relative to the charge and not to the minister occupying it. Their argument in essence was that the stipend due to the charge had, for many years, been set too low.

I was hugely embarrassed. At no time throughout my

ministries had I sought financial advantage. Quite the reverse had always been the case. Both in Penicuik and in Croftfoot, where I could influence decisions of the board, as for instance over manse expenditure, I had rigorously resisted any expenditure that could be deemed to be to our advantage as a manse family. Indeed, we sometimes went too far for our own good as, for instance, where we allowed the Congregational Board to buy paint for redecorating a much-neglected public room. I insisted that I then applied the paint myself, thus avoiding further expense. I had been ever vigilant that no one could ever assert that my family or I benefited from my enthusiasm for meaningful Christian stewardship. In a word, I would accept no financial advantage. Now I was being confronted by proposals that I could not influence in any way. The proposed increase looked totally outrageous, and I was unhappily certain that this would be the perception in some quarters at least. All I could do was brace myself and await the reaction. Within the Congregational Board, I have to say there was no discernible adverse response. Amongst the immediate leaders of the congregation there was a sense of pride that their minister was now being properly valued. My intimates were of the view that I was worth every penny and more. This sense of being valued was given further expression to by a decision of the board to meet an invitation from the Maintenance of the Ministry Committee for the Congregational Board to make a contribution on behalf of their minister to a new Insured Ministers' Fund. The board, having been invited to offer a minimum of one hundred pounds per year, determined to offer five hundred pounds per year and did.

On 12th March 1979, our Annual Stated Meeting took place, and this meeting throughout my years at Croftfoot had been characterised by warmth and good feeling. There had ever been a business menu that had won admiration and applause. This year's menu offered the same good fare already mentioned – that is, the thirty per cent increase in congregational receipts. All our business was attended to in the usual capable manner with conveners and treasurers of standing committees offering thoughtful and good contributions. We concluded the formal business and moved on to what had become a tradition, namely an informal questions and answers session. One young married woman in the congregation, who had set her face firmly against the 'Give As You Earn' scheme and had registered her distaste for it, chose to speak. She challenged the fairness of the huge increase in the minister's stipend when she and many others like her had to make do with the usual inflationary increases, which came yearly. This lady was not an office bearer and could not be expected to be aware of information which could have changed her thinking and her blunt manner of expressing it. What was infinitely disturbing to me was the diffused rumblings occasioned by surreptitious foot movements. The meeting consisted almost entirely of fellow office bearers, and a fair number were registering their dissent in a manner not open to detection. I felt it most unworthy of them and, once I had further corroboration of an emerging attitude, I would know how to respond. Meantime, my assessment was that my time was swiftly running out. The chances were my ministry at Croftfoot would soon end. These underground expressions of opposition helped to confirm the feeling I sensed from an earlier congregational conference in February. There, for the first time, I had detected a slight withdrawal of enthusiasm and support for our annual visitation. There was a growing malaise and the signals seemed to be: 'Dear minister, thus far and no further!' My people, if elements of the Kirk Session and Congregational Board were to be believed, had travelled far enough. I had sensed also that my closest and most supportive office bearers were somewhat beleaguered. I had no means of knowing if adverse comments had come their way, but I had the feeling that some of them had come under pressure and were feeling it.

By and large, few office bearers would have connected any fall-off in enthusiasm with the Kirk Session intervention made the previous winter, but it had proved a rallying point for the disaffected and there was, I judged, the beginning of a cancer gnawing at our wellbeing. One of our elders, whose son, also an organist and a close friend of our recently departed organist, introduced a note of acrimony in the manner of his resignation. Our Kirk Session, in acceding to his resignation, did so in a manner which hinted at a measure of understanding with his going. This intelligence, coupled with other evident signs of weariness in the work, convinced me that I had led my folk as far as they were happy to travel.

I called a special Kirk Session meeting and intimated my decision to demit my charge as from 30th June 1979. I was deeply saddened because I was conceding that my approach to ministry was destined to failure. I had now led two quite different congregations in the direction of attaining a worthy corporate as well as individual witness. My task had been to expose them to the cost of discipleship. Most of our people, if they were being open and honest, would allow that their true condition was enquirer after the faith and not as great exemplars of it. In that position I was most happy to stand with them. In all honesty I could not dilute my own understanding of the privileges and the charges of the faith in order to preside over a static body characterised by a 'thus far and no further' philosophy. My consternation was heightened further when I considered the wider malaise of the Church. If my congregation was deemed strong in the ways open to measurement, what did that say of the plight of the Church in general? To dare to ventilate the subject in this way would in no manner endear me to my fellow ministers as they struggled to come to terms with their own situation. Nor would my position meet with a welcoming resonance from the seat of power at 121 George Street. I was thus led to conclude that I could not offer myself for further ministry. Two such experiences of ministry such as I had conducted should be sufficient for one lifetime.

The Kirk Session received my intimation in stunned silence and with a large degree of disbelief. My assistant looked genuinely sorrowful. It was left to our senior elder, Albert Foster, who had a reputation as a consummate public speaker but also as a man who spoke too long, to reply. Albert was in his middle seventies and had been a retired elder throughout my ministry but we both held each other in high regard. Albert indicated that he could speak confidently for the whole session in expressing his sorrow at my going. He went on to say things in my favour, which no man should hear, and therefore will remain unrecorded. Suffice to say great regret was expressed and I shared their regret too.

I duly intimated my decision to Glasgow Presbytery after I had visited the Rev. Dr Andrew Herron and had endeavoured to explain my position. Dr Herron had invited me in the past to share lunch with him at the Glasgow Art Club in Bath Street, his usual lunchtime haunt. I was being summed-up during the two occasions I had been extended this courtesy even if, as was the case, Presbytery matters were on the lunchtime agenda. I, in truth, was always wary of Andrew Herron, who was a manipulator of Church affairs par excellence. Dr Herron listened with interest to my explanation of the need for my demission as I saw it. When I interconnected my experience as being applicable to both my congregations, I observed an immediate change of attitude in this man long experienced in listening to, and counselling so many of, my colleagues in their various difficulties and traumas.

I was being pigeonholed. I could sense he now felt he better understood. I felt he was light years away from understanding and I was soon to be confirmed in my view. 'Now,' said Dr Herron, 'Do you not realise, Hugh, that if you proceed in this manner, you will put your whole career at risk?' I bristled slightly at this and responded that my career mattered little to me, as I had always understood myself as being called. Andrew Herron had all the confirmation he wanted from our meeting, and so had I. He outlined the necessary procedure, indicating that a committee of the Presbytery would meet with me to ascertain the relevant facts. Dr Herron advised that the rather bland-sounding, and all-embracing phrase, 'for personal reasons', would cover my reason for demission. So it was that on 8th May 1979, Glasgow Presbytery received my request to demit my Pastoral Charge at Croftfoot as from 30th June 1979 and, after due process, assented to my request.

In addressing the Presbytery I acknowledged my gratitude for the friendship and support of so many of my fellow office bearers over the years we had served together. I thanked also, of course, my people for all their work and witness throughout my time with them. I concluded with reference to my need for demission, as I saw it, and alluded to the vexation it had caused me. I explained that I could not find it in my heart to adjust or compromise with what I held to be the message given me as a preacher of the Gospel. I know, and have found, as we all have found, that God is good and that we have been purchased at great price. I concluded that we owe everything to God in Christ, and our response in our worship, our service and in our giving, is our only 'reasonable service'.

Some three weeks later, the Presbytery newspaper, *The Bush*, reported as usual on the Presbytery business that had occurred on the night of my demission and there was an addendum to the report in these terms:

'FAREWELL'

Was there anything else?

Yes. A sad thing. The minister of Croftfoot adhered to his intention to demit his charge, even after the Presbytery special committee had met with him. The Presbytery was not told the details of why he was going or what he was now going to do. It was said that 'his care of the membership was of the highest standard and that he had taken Croftfoot away ahead in the 'Give As You Earn' league. In that way too, as Convener of Stewardship and Budget, he had led the Presbytery the best way: by example. God bless you, Hugh.

This was a kind and welcome final word from some of my colleagues.

The week following my appearance at Presbytery, the local and national newspapers picked up on my pastoral letter in the May issue of *Gleanings*. I had used our magazine as the medium for communicating with all our members and, in my letter, I explained the reasons behind my imminent departure. The press seized upon this letter and we at the manse had quite a torrid time fielding enquiries from the press and, indeed, BBC Radio Scotland. There followed the usual speculation. Was there anything more to my decision? Would a minister depart from his settled and harmonious congregation on the basis of what I had stated? There was heightened press interest from Friday 18th May until Monday 21st May. Our congregation at worship on Sunday saw the *Glasgow Herald* reporter, Tom Shields, moving around the congregation seeking information that might be newsworthy. We were well pleased when they seemingly concluded that the intelligence available was accurate and that beyond this they had no other story.

As soon as I had advised my people of my impending resignation, then, and then only, did I turn my thoughts as to how I would continue to provide for my family. I consulted the usual employment vacancies' columns, prepared to consider anything immediately available which did not clash with my moral scruples. An advertisement under the heading of Barclays Life Assurance, linking that company with Barclays Bank, caught my eye. The vacancy required a financially literate candidate to promote the sale of executive pension schemes to likely purchasers. There would be, I discovered, a guaranteed income provided during the first three months, covering the training and induction period. I applied and was accepted. My new career move would commence as soon as I was freed from my Church commitment. So far so good, I thought. At the same time, we knew we would have to vacate our manse by the end of June. I set in train the sale of our holiday home at 3 Sandringham Terrace, Largs. Our flat was deemed a most desirable one which, incidentally, Andrew Herron had come to know about, and about which in a jocular fashion had expressed envy. As we anticipated, we had no difficulty in securing the sale of the flat. Thus empowered, we began the search for a suitable home. Rena and Douglas fastened onto a likely property located quite nearby in Brownside Road, Cambuslang. They inspected the six-roomed, semi-detached villa and were much taken by the spacious apartments and particularly so with the extensive garden grounds within which the house was set. They registered their very keen interest that Saturday morning with the owner and indicated that I would in all probability visit that same afternoon. Sensing the need for haste and a quick decision, I inspected the property that afternoon and met with the appropriately named owner, Mr Kirk. I was delighted with my family's earlier gained good impression of the house and there and then I offered to meet Mr Kirk's asking price. We shook hands on the deal and both parties expressed satisfaction at this early outcome. Our solicitor acted expeditiously and, very rapidly indeed, we had the prospective security of a roof over our heads. May I add that my office bearers at Croftfoot, being aware that we appeared to be heading for a housing crisis, had insisted that beyond 1st July we would be most welcome to occupy the manse until we were able to make alternative arrangements. This gesture of goodwill and concern we very much appreciated. In the event, we did not require to resort to it and we moved timeously in tune with my scheduled Church departure.

I conducted my valedictory service on Sunday 27th May 1979 and my parting message to my people was that they remain strong and committed to the faith and strive together to achieve great things into the future to the greater glory of God. I bade them a tender farewell. After the service, courtesies of appreciation and affection were exchanged and I was presented with a most generous cheque from the congregation, subscribed to by so many of my fellow members. Throughout the month of May and into June, I was to be the recipient of innumerable letters. Many came from members who felt they had particular need to communicate on the basis of past shared experiences, sometimes of happiness, but often of sadness. Others again wished simply to record their appreciation of my ministry in their midst. Because of the press exposure, I received letters from total strangers who sometimes recounted their own experiences, but who, in all cases, wished my family and me well and commended us to God. A fair number of my colleagues, particularly from the Presbytery, wrote in supporting and kindly tones and expressed regret at my going but in all cases respecting my decision. Deeply saddened but totally resolute, I departed from Croftfoot, and from the ordained service of the Church forever.

After a period of eleven extremely busy and, in many ways, rewarding years, how had I met the challenge of my call? From the outset I had been powerfully persuaded that my life up to the time of my sensing God's call had provided me with a rich and varied tapestry of experience. This, I was convinced, should be employed in God's service. Until my mature years I had been a doubter. I knew about doubt and I felt that I would encounter much of it throughout my coming ministry. My best evangelising tool would be that I had once stood where so many in the Church still stood. The challenge for me was to provide insights and experience operating within the interplay of the Holy Spirit that would lead men and women into all truth. Truth, therefore, was to be the central plank of my ministry. I would endeavour, God helping me, to live it and I would challenge for it. In theological terms, this would cause me to challenge all dogma and all doctrines that looked for a comfortable, thoughtless accommodation. In my days of doubt I had challenged, intellectually, dogma and doctrine, and had, even so, been won for the faith. The lesson, in my case, was that where dogma and adherence to some doctrines impinge upon and grate with your God-given intelligence, and tend to separate you from the faith, then regard them less.

For example, the doctrine of the virgin birth is not of the essence of the faith. It is an accretion. More than that, for untold thousands it is an impediment that obscures the reality of the nature of the faith. We profess our belief in Jesus Christ incarnate. We respond to Jesus of Nazareth who went about this world doing good. We are inspired by His life, not by the manner of its beginning, and by His love and devotion to all mankind, and by His death and not least the manner of it. It is as we respond to our understanding of what manner of man He was that we are gripped and held, captivated and transformed. This is the stuff of faith, not wearisome endless debates about the background of Christmas. Look at Jesus' life and His prescription, and it is precious little wonder that they crucified Him. This is the manner of Man into whose service I had so freely given myself. If our Lord were a seeker after truth then what better example could one follow? Truth exists, of course, at so many levels. There is the truth about oneself that might be most unpalatable as opposed to objective truth concerning a defined issue.

From the beginning, I wished to challenge my people with the concept of truthfulness. Truth is a virtue. To be possessed of it or to strive after it is a worthy preoccupation. For the Christian, the examined life should be an imperative. Do I believe? Do I truly believe? Our belief can be measured by our actions and so I came to understand that to expose a man or woman's true conviction you could apply some simple, straightforward tests. Worship, service and giving – the tests of stewardship would provide insight into the spiritual condition.

How could we talk about sacrificial service unless we were prepared to sacrifice? Jesus Christ was the Man for others, who laid down His life for others and He inspired others in extremis so to do. *'Greater love hath no man than this; that a man lay down his life for a friend!'* That is an honouring statement and an infinitely greater attainment when accomplished. This example of human sacrifice is reflective of someone who has journeyed far up a high mountain. Most of us are stranded low down on the nursery slopes. Yet we call ourselves followers of Christ! Is there any real truth in the claim? My experience had convinced me that there was a connection between what a person believed and how such a person handled his or her money. What mature, loving Christian could cavil with the notion, 'Lavishly you have received, lavishly give!' This then was the examination I set before my congregations and, by inference, the wider Church. Simply being generous and thoughtful towards the caring work of the Church reveals only a little about a person's grasp of the faith. The impulsion towards committed worship and sharing of talents should be the more difficult to achieve. If to be generous tells you only a little concerning the spiritual condition, what does meanness tell you? I had ministered for eleven years with evangelical zeal to establish this message and allow our people the liberty to move upward from the nursery slopes within whose grasp they were held. I, in effect, had been advised, 'You ask too much.' I think not. We, as a Church, ask too little and we throttle the lovely, living spirit of Christ in our midst. It amounts to a 21st century re-enactment of the crucifixion. These thoughts encapsulate the reasons behind my withdrawal from the parish ministry, and in this I was merely giving expression to the good counsel, *'To thine own self be true'*.

Chapter Eleven

I had now been returned to secular society with the responsibility of providing for my wife and two teenage members of the family. Douglas, who was now seventeen, had just completed his first year's study in the Law Faculty at Glasgow University where he was pursuing an Accountancy Degree. Gillian had, on 2nd July, reached sweet sixteen and was working towards Highers at Stonelaw High. Rena was still engaged in her part-time work with the Pharmaceutical Society. The family was totally in tune with my decision to terminate my ministry. Being children of the manse had been no great thing as far as they were concerned. They both quite looked forward to being free of the 'goldfish bowl' syndrome that inevitably belongs to manse life.

I had clutched at the opportunity of immediate employment and my long involvement in matters financial, coupled with an innate aptitude for figures, gave me cause to believe that the work in prospect would be interesting. After a few days under the introductory tutelage of the Glasgow branch manager and the handing over to me of masses of pensions' literature, I was sent off to the Barclays Bank establishment at Knutsford. This was to be my place of induction. The course, which lasted a mere four weeks, was designed to teach us all we needed to know in order to successfully sell the pensions' products that the company had to offer. I found myself in a group of fourteen trainees who had been garnered from various occupations. They were eager to assimilate all the techniques on offer to enable them to become adept salespeople. In all this, I was experiencing the beginnings of a sense of distaste. The underlying theme of the lectures was motivation. The question was repeatedly raised: 'What is your motivation? – List your six most desirable wants!' The total emphasis was on the sales force securing sales sufficient to enable all their dreams of riches to be fulfilled. My fellow trainees seemed to think this all quite wonderful. They could hardly wait to put all the offered insights into practice. The lecturer's ace card, and it is one well known to all participants within the insurance industry, was the mantra K.I.S.S. 'Keep it simple, stupid!' What had I involved myself with? Day by day I grew more troubled at the flow of teaching material that came my way. I had the temerity to ask the lecturer about the quality and comparative status of the company's financial products as compared with the offerings of other competitors. I was frostily advised that it was no part of our responsibility to pursue that kind of question. 'Just,' he said, 'concentrate on selling our products on the basis of the information we provide.' We were introduced to the techniques of so-called, cold telephone calling, drawing up lists of potential clients to approach. When they responded, we were told to indicate that we were from Barclays Bank, thus triggering a sense of acceptability and trust flowing from the use of the name. Nothing had been suggested to the effect that I would be required to spend time thumbing through the telephone directory and engaging small-time business people on their need for making pension provision. By now I had a very clear grasp of the stratagem the company deployed. The induction course was designed to produce, from among the fourteen participants, an eager, bright-eyed and bushy-tailed sales force which, with their hearts set upon untold riches, would utilise all means at their disposal to sell pensions. They would, of course, start with themselves – that would be easy. It would also be comparatively easy to sell pensions to their families. Beyond this, they might reasonably expect to sell pensions to their friends, all of which was grist to the mill. The insurance company doubtless knew from long commercial experience just how profitable was the payback from this sort of enterprise. I now saw quite clearly why they reckoned that I could be paid a guaranteed income for the first three months. They were confident, again, no doubt from actuarial experience, that I would have written sufficient policies in that time, issuing from an explosion of enthusiasm, to more than meet their outgoings on my behalf. I was desperately now looking for an exit.

For two or three weeks I dutifully pursued my training programme by telephoning around and securing appointments. I then met with potential clients and explained the undoubted benefits belonging to the personal pension plan I was proposing. I was not certain that I had sufficient appetite for the successful closing gambit of K.I.S.S. As it was, I had not taken out a personal pension plan; I had not encouraged my family or friends to support me in my new role as pensions consultant. In fact, when I decided that resignation was imperative, I must have been Barclay Life Assurance Company's worst ever investment. I had not written a single policy in almost two months in their employ. I was pleased to be through with the entire ill-starred enterprise. What did not please me was that I was now unemployed.

In order to maintain my national insurance contributions' record, it was necessary that I register with the Social Security Department in Rutherglen. This is, I avow, an experience much to be avoided. I took my place in a long straggling queue of hopeless and defeated-looking and sometimes drugged individuals who were awaiting attention. The line duly eased forward and I was called to a window position to state my business. I was quickly advised that since I had left my employment voluntarily, Barclays having confirmed this, then I was not eligible for unemployment benefit until the passing of six weeks. On the positive side, I was advised, I should appear meantime each week and register my continued status and in return my national insurance stamp would be credited. I left that establishment with the assured conviction that I would not be returning. Their stamps, at the price, I did not wish for, and their unemployment benefit, we would do without.

I might have been unemployed but I was not inactive. In the winter of the previous year, whilst still at Croftfoot, I had commenced a BA degree course with the Open University. The course was a part-time one and the gathering of the six credits comprising the degree requirement could take six years of study. Much more happily, from my point of view, ministers of religion wishing to take the degree could be, and mostly were, granted three credits towards their degree. I had been studying for the first of my three required credits over the winter and into the spring and, with the foundation course credit gained, I was primed to embark on the second required credit. However, not being employed, I had the time and the opportunity to commence the two remaining subjects simultaneously and so aim to complete the degree in just two years of study. Rena had also decided to enrol on the same course and her professional qualifications permitted the granting of two credits. So there we were, both of us in our mid-forties, keen and committed to studying within the OU. Studying was a pleasurable and diverting interest but the altogether more serious matter of our livelihood had to be addressed. I was now decidedly suspicious about offering myself without reserve into the job market. An answer, however, had to be found.

Rena could seek full-time employment and the benefit would be obvious. However, it came to us that we could overcome our difficulties by deciding to go into business, and what better business could we consider than pharmacy. Rena had the requisite skills and, allied to which, she had an outgoing and caring disposition admirably suited to retail pharmacy. I, on the other hand, had a secure grip of figures, statistics and a good knowledge of accounts. I could administer such a business and Rena could professionally conduct it. I needed gainful employment and Rena was prepared to undertake full-time employment. We had ever been a team in the ministry. We could comfortably be a team again. With these embryonic plans forming, we set about finding a business. We resorted to the *Pharmaceutical Journal* and our eyes latched upon a likely prospect. A small family business was for sale in Toryglen, Glasgow, and, as it happened, its owner, Mr Bill Melrose, was known to us both. Rena had the added advantage, given by her role with the Pharmaceutical Society, of having visited the business on a number of occasions. I knew Bill socially from our time formerly spent together as members of the pharmacy badminton club. We arranged a business meeting with Bill and his wife, who helped him run the pharmacy. Bill had reached sixty-five and had suffered a heart attack, hence his concern now for retirement. We had, of course, bought our new house in Cambuslang and had provided cash for the bulk of the purchase price. But even so, we had conserved a good sum of capital and this prudence and management was now to show benefit. We agreed a figure with Bill in respect of goodwill and an appropriate amount for stock, subject to valuation. The deal was concluded and after all the legal niceties we took possession of the business on 1st

February 1980. The purchase of the business had taken up all of our resources, such that, when unexpectedly called upon by the telephone company to produce a modest one hundred pounds, we were literally broke. Providentially, that very same day, Thursday 31st January, we were with the Melroses on their last day of business for the stocktaking handover and, at 5.30 p.m., the Melroses handed over the cash takings of the afternoon, which had been out-with the stocktaking calculation. That cash spoke of solvency on the day and we were never to look back. I had chosen to leave Croftfoot without the merest regard to the decision's financial implication upon our future wellbeing. The fifty-five per cent increase that had created a measure of displeasure in some quarters with mutterings of 'It's all right for him' had scandalised me by the suggestion that I might have been angling for financial gain, and so I was not unhappy to leave behind my 'grossly inflated' stipend within months of having received it. Now, some seven months on from that decision, we were in possession of a new business that, we were to discover within a few more weeks, was to provide me with an income in excess of the same 'grossly inflated' Church stipend and, moreover, since Rena and I were equal partners, Rena was also in receipt of a similar sum. In purely human terms, it could be said, if I were interested, that I had made a good career move. Our newly acquired pharmacy had been a well-conducted family business that the Melroses had built up over twenty-five years of worthy community service. When we took possession we had determined that Rena very properly would take care of the very busy dispensary and that my task would be looking after the shopfront sales. For many days and weeks ahead I must have driven Rena to the point of distraction with my requests for clarification about this product and that, and not least as to their whereabouts in the shopfront. The customers, having been used to a male proprietor for so many years, frequently mistook me for the pharmacist, but they came in time to see where the power lay and very soon relied on Rena for good advice. Gillian joined us from the very beginning as the Saturday girl and so the ethos of 'family business' was well grounded. Toryglen, at the time of our arrival, was served by two pharmacies. The large pharmacy chain, Gordon Drummond, provided services in opposition to us and I immediately grasped that even in the short term the local community could not comfortably support two pharmacies. Both businesses were of a similar size and both were vulnerable. Even allowing for the disparate resources available to each business, I was determined that we would prevail. I was certain that we could offer a better service and that by displaying care and consideration to our customers we could retain their custom and loyalty. Gordon Drummond, on the other hand, was at the distinct disadvantage of being somewhat impersonal, which is the price multiples must pay in the marketplace.

We were at a competitive disadvantage to the multiple in terms of pricing, and we constantly, in the early days, had to resort to the cash and carry as a means of securing certain lines of merchandise. Over time, we found the challenge exhilarating and we carefully monitored our performance month by month. At the outset, in the course of our business shopping sprees on our Tuesday half-day, we would dine within the Makro complex. Then we noticed that we could dine in a better quality place until, after a time, we could afford to be selective in our choice of good dining. Business had certainly brought its own rewards. Business was also providing me with the opportunity of being of useful service to the community in terms of their physical welfare, now that I had withdrawn from the arena where my services could be of spiritual benefit.

Rena and I had become members of Trinity Church, Cambuslang, where the Rev. John Cubie ministered most effectively and with wide acceptance. By June of 1980, almost exactly a year since my last pulpit appearance, I was prevailed upon to conduct worship at St Paul's Church, also in Cambuslang, where at short notice the need for pulpit supply had arisen. My having taken this service seemingly led to the understanding that I was available for pulpit supply and I was approached to conduct worship at Dennistoun Central in Glasgow on 3rd August. I duly did so and was invited to occupy the pulpit for the three further unfilled Sundays in August. I found much satisfaction in being, after a fashion, back in harness, and the appreciation expressed allowed me to think that possibly, in some manner, I could still be of service to the Church. It was against this background that

I read an advertisement for an industrial chaplain at Sullom Voe in the Orkneys. After much thought and careful consideration with Rena, we both agreed that we would be open to making the adjustments necessary, and indeed the sacrifices required, in the event of my being appointed to this post. The new position being created would call for robust ministry in a geographically demanding and remote location. As an expression of my commitment to the faith, I believed I should offer myself for this service. I applied to the Church and Ministry Committee at 121 George Street, which would make the appointment. I was invited to furnish them with three referees and this I duly did after approaching three good friends in the ministry. All readily agreed to offer references. The committee appointed a date and I travelled to Edinburgh and, at the appropriate time, I was invited to appear for interview. The Rev. Dr David Whiteford convened the committee and he was flanked by Rev. George Lugton, secretary of the Church and Ministry Committee and by his assistant secretary, Rev. Tom Balfour. Two or three other ministers and a couple of lay members made up the remainder. I was instantly struck by the strict, icy and formal manner of their preliminary questioning. I had entered a hostile environment, and I was at a loss to even guess as to what had occasioned the sharpness and brusqueness of their questions. Pre-eminent in all this was one particular committee member. He had the reputation of being a man not to be trifled with. I was aware of his bullying and aggressive manner and how it served to cow those with whom he might be in dispute. His tone towards me was hectoring. He found an ally in another member, who was a man who could not be said to be possessed of a gracious and kindly manner. I gained the impression that he thought he was addressing subordinates. The secretary tapped his pencil occasionally against his notepad and said not a word. They questioned me about what I was presently doing in terms of employment. I judged they already had that information. Then, quite out of the blue, they asked me about my attitude towards Roman Catholics. I bristled and replied that there was nothing whatsoever in my entire ministry which could have justified such a question. Thereupon, one of the laymen present, whom I knew from my time at Dalkeith Presbytery, and who was widely known to be highly opinionated and who aired his views regularly at General Assemblies, pitched in with what he took to be the final word of the interview, 'I have heard enough,' he said. Strangely enough, so had I! The interview was swiftly concluded and, as I made my way homeward, I was in no need of the confirmation that arrived, first post, next morning. This experience caused me great misgiving. How could a committee of the Church of Scotland behave in this manner towards a candidate they had invited to be interviewed? If this was but a reflection of the nature of our National Church then I felt great shame on its behalf.

The year drew to its close. Rena and I had maintained our study at the Open University, and on 8th December 1980

I was awarded the degree of Bachelor of Arts – a nice note on which to end the year. My unhappy Edinburgh interview apart, I was more and more open to the thought that I could still make a contribution to the witness of the Church. This was a radical change of thinking but I suppose preaching does get into the blood and serving in this manner would be a vindication of the faith within. I wondered whether I should begin the search for a suitable congregation, at which point I saw that, in nearby East Kilbride, a struggling Church Extension Charge was vacant and was seeking an experienced minister. Such charges, by their nature, were both demanding and rewarding. The Home Board was the relevant authority and the board was responsible for the appointment. Here again there was a 121 George Street involvement. I drew confidence from the knowledge that this committee was not composed of people from the Church and Ministry Committee of fairly recent and bitter experience. I applied, furnished the requisite references, and awaited their response. I was selected for the shortlist and presented myself for interview by the committee of the Home Board, as I thought. I had immediate reason to think again. At precisely 11.20 a.m. on Friday 20th February 1981, I was invited to leave off my coat by the Rev. Tom Balfour, before meeting with the interviewing committee. As I was being shown along to the interview room, I queried of Tom Balfour why he, a representative of the Church and Ministry Committee, should be present. He quickly explained that a new committee structure had just been put in place and all interviews involving the Home Board would have joint representation with Church and Ministry members, and vice versa. I could not believe that I was about to be propelled into an interview involving men for whom I now had a large measure of distaste. The secretary of the Home Board was the Rev. Dr Ian Doyle, whom I had met informally a number of times at Crieff Hydro and I always found him to be a pleasantly mannered, friendly and capable man. I had anticipated meeting with his committee in his presence. Had I known of the new construction with Church and Ministry involvement, I would not have presented myself as a candidate. As it was, I was led into the room and there, apart from my previous chief inquisitor, was Rev. George Lugton, inscrutable as ever, and three or four other members from my previous encounter. This group was nicely balanced by the group representing the Home Board element of this new committee. I noticed immediately that Dr Doyle was not present. The interview proceeded. Members of the Home Board contingent asked me a series of relevant questions and all their questioning was entirely appropriate and offered in a clear and pleasant manner. The settled, friendly atmosphere was interrupted by a contribution from my chief inquisitor, who wanted to know why I had elected to apply for the nearby East Kilbride charge and not for a similar vacant charge available in Aberdeen. I responded, indicating that I had been unaware of the Aberdeen situation. The implication of his question was related to the fact, no doubt, that our family business could be better conducted if we were located in East

Kilbride and not Aberdeen. My inquisitor, on this reasoning, had seemingly forgotten that, months before, I had expressed willingness to travel to Sullom Voe and that I had been rejected. He was, with his line of questioning, pursuing an agenda of which I knew nothing. Meanwhile, the Rev. George Lugton, eyes averted, continued to drum with his pencil and said nothing. The interview progressed to its conclusion and, as I left, I had the sense that I had interviewed well, and that, Church and Ministry Committee apart, I had a good chance of being appointed. I did not, though, underestimate the input of some members present. Next morning, I did not receive a letter. Indeed, three weeks passed before I was to receive the communication, which expressed commiserations at my non-appointment and wished me well. It was reported to me by a friend located in 121 George Street that when the committee considered my candidature they divided half for me and half against. Now there was a surprise! What was more of a surprise was the intelligence passed to me that the absent Dr Doyle had instructed that, if it came to a vote, he favoured me. It had come to a vote apparently and I was not favoured. The delay of some three weeks in informing me, I simply could not comment on, other than to say that perhaps I was first reserve.

I mentioned much earlier how I had been made aware of the vagaries of the selection system touching on church vacancies and how resort was made to men of great experience in the assessment of suitable candidates for particular charges. Dr Andrew Herron was deemed a fount of all wisdom in this respect within Glasgow Presbytery and even further afield. By the same token, the 'mandarins' at 121 George Street had a similar reputation and standing. They could both make and break. As I reflected on this and coupled this knowledge with the thought that I might soon wish to apply for a charge, I was powerfully persuaded that 121 George Street had to be worth a visit. I had good grounds to think that the 'powers that be' knew something about me that oddly enough had escaped me. What could this be? Was it simply a matter of reining in a minister who followed an agenda unacceptable to them? If so, could they be explicit?

The secretary to the Church and Ministry Committee was understood, on different counts, to be a most powerful and influential minister within the Church. Many saw him as having the role of pastor to the minister and undoubtedly many errant or weak or unhappy or incompetent ministers would either need or seek his counsel. I was not about to seek his counsel, but rather a face-to-face meeting with him. I communicated with him and we agreed to meet at his office. So far as I was concerned, this was a meeting to which I would bring with me a degree of tension. The stakes as I saw them were high. As we met, I quickly laid before George Lugton my great concern. I was highly suspicious that if enquiry were made concerning me in regard to any Church application I might make into the future, then information detrimental to me would be passed on. Simply put, I would be blackballed! I wished George Lugton in my presence to disclose any such information that I might take account of it and refute it. I judged he knew, and I certainly knew, that the conduct of the two interviews involving his committee and me contained undertones that needed explanation. I was urging upon him that he disclose any such information. George Lugton was at pains to assure me that he greatly respected my personal integrity and that my work had been honouring, and he wished to stress that, so far as he was concerned, I could be confident that he would not be implicated in any idea of blackballing. We had a fraught hour or so together and I questioned him on his lack of input into the two interviews which had so disturbed me. His defence was that he, as the secretary, had a different role. I let Mr Lugton know that I was by no means convinced by the give and take of our present meeting, but I would be totally vigilant into the future, should I ever have occasion to feel that I had been improperly represented based on information flowing from 121 George Street. As I prepared to depart, George Lugton was by now displaying an understanding and friendly manner and, as we edged towards his door, in a spirit of friendship, he suggested that his door would be forever open to me. This sounded just a touch formulaic to me, and I retorted 'George, this has been my first visit to your office and, so far as I am concerned, it will be my last.' I did not view myself as someone in need of his counsel. I had suspected a grave injustice perpetrated against me and

I wished no repetition. As we reached the door, George Lugton offered me his hand and as we shook hands, he said, 'Hugh, a word of advice – you should be more careful in your choice of friends!' I was dumbstruck but recovered sufficiently to exchange a knowing glance, and then I was off. In that final moment I now much better understood why so hostile a committee had confronted me. One of my three friends had been not at all friendly! To the two friends among my three referees who were entirely blameless I tender and declare my continuous respect and friendship. Throughout the time in question they made their regard for me plain, and I have retained the evidence of that regard. They are, therefore, men of good conscience, and if they read these words their eyes need in no manner be averted. To the third of the trio I say this. I had held you in high esteem, despite our perceived differences of temperament and emphasis on ministry. I had thought that our friendship was mutually secure. By your resort to an unkind and, I have to believe, totally misleading representation of my character, you have not alone done me an injustice, but gravely demeaned yourself. If you had properly held reservations concerning me, you should not have so willingly agreed to offer a reference on my behalf. I have to believe that Christ's cause cannot be advanced by conduct of this nature.

Chapter Twelve

Having cleared the air with George Lugton, I was now able to think about applying for a new charge. The parish of Buchanan and Drymen was vacant at this time and I chose to make application. It was a happy coincidence that at this time I was the regular occupant of the pulpit at St Andrew's, Motherwell, and so had, as it were, a secure platform from which to be heard. I had been invited to take pulpit supply at this vacant charge on Palm Sunday and again the following Sunday; Easter Day. The good people of St Andrew's appeared content with the temporary incumbent and invited me to prolong my stay for the duration of their vacancy. The Buchanan and Drymen vacancy people visited on Sunday 10th May. Within the strange orbit of chatter and communication attaching to vacancy matters, one of my former elders from Penicuik South, who was called to the ministry during my time there, now passed on some news. My friend, the Rev. Bill Bryden, knew the Interim Moderator at Buchanan and Drymen and from their conversation Bill had elicited the information that the committee had been much taken by my ministry. I was, apparently, the front-runner and they would be returning the following Sunday to confirm their stance. They did indeed return and after the service they sought an interview with me. I was quite taken by the representatives they had commissioned and the interview progressed well until one elderly member, noting the comparative brevity of my two previous ministries, enquired about how long I would stay with them if elected. He went on to explain that their two previous ministries had lasted over forty years each. I could not, of course, hope to compete with this longevity, but I well understood the thrust of the question. The committee desired that I give an undertaking to remain in their midst for a long time. Had I wished to engineer an accommodation of their hopes then I knew exactly how I should proceed. This I could not do. It would be both unfair and false to the congregation and to myself to give any such undertaking. I explained as gently as I could that in God's providence I could be led to minister in their midst in keeping with their best hopes but I could not in good conscience give such a promise. I had cast a slight shadow and I feared all would not now be well. My fear was confirmed when, as the committee were filing out and expressing their appreciation for the meeting, the last man to leave, a solicitor, I had learned during our meeting, indicated that a reference I had made about older men in the ministry was somewhat snide. Now, snide is an ugly word and there had been nothing I could recall having said in the course of the interview that would have merited such a description. That, however, was not the point. This formidable man had clearly set his heart against my ever becoming his minister and he was obviously well positioned to secure that end. My past

171

intelligence about the intentions of the committee was no longer valid. Curiously enough, in the context of the vacancy at Buchanan and Drymen, I received a letter from a most refined lady member of the visiting committee who wished, as she put it, to 'thank you once again for your courtesy in receiving us. It has been a long time since I found a service so wholly pleasing.' She indicated that, with thirty applicants, it was going to be quite a task to come to a final decision. She concluded that whatever happened she hoped that I would soon be settled in a charge where I, together with my family, would have many happy years. This was a kind sentiment and I appreciated her letter very much. Through the grapevine, I was advised that, to the disappointment of the Interim Moderator, the Vacancy Committee of Buchanan and Drymen, by the smallest of margins, decided on the 'safer' of the two candidates under final consideration. With the concerns that they displayed, they had undoubtedly made the correct choice. I was aware, though, that my 'form' would be a factor to be overcome when confronting any future Vacancy Committee. I continued to preach at St Andrew's until the beginning of July when I took a break and arranged a special holiday with Rena in anticipation of our silver wedding anniversary the following year. I arranged that we would fly to New York, spend four days, and then crown our return home by travelling on the Queen Elizabeth II.

Before setting off for New York I had received numerous requests from members of St Andrew's to consider applying for the charge. The Vacancy Committee had remained undecided about their choice of minister for some months and many voices had suggested that they should look to myself. This the committee could not do without an initiative from me. Rena and I had both been much taken by the warmth and open friendliness of the congregation. It was a struggling church community that lacked a good opinion of itself. It was ever cast in the role of underdog and had come to believe this reputation as apt and fitting. I had to ask myself whether, if I were ever to become their minister, I could accommodate such low expectations, and whether to unsettle these would be harmful to the happy family atmosphere that pervaded despite the obvious fact that they were, by another measure, in the doldrums. The reality was that preaching in their midst was a real pleasure and their response was ever warm and appreciative.

Whilst on holiday, the way forward became clear to me, and I decided that I should make formal application immediately upon my return. I did so and since the committee did not require to 'hear' me, I was rapidly approached by Mrs Ann Kerr, the clerk to the Vacancy Committee, on its behalf, and I, with the utmost pleasure, responded. Meantime, I would not occupy their pulpit again until I became their minister.

All these developments meant that I would require to make various adjustments touching on our business life. Sawers Chemist was now trading very securely and the developments that I had foreseen had come to pass. Gordon Drummond had been constantly squeezed in terms of its customer base and to our obvious relief ceased trading. This factor led to an impressive strengthening of our business. With my imminent withdrawal from the front line we had to make staff adjustments. I had been much impressed by the nature and character of one of our customers, Mrs Susan Creamer, and to her astonishment I approached her with a view to part-time employment with us. Susan was surprised, to say the least, but very happy indeed to accept our offer. With the closure of Gordon Drummond, Rena, who had been aware of the fine qualities of one of their staff members, Mrs Margaret Wilson, contacted the lady, who instantly rejoiced to join forces with us. Both these ladies were to become good and valued friends and served within our family business throughout our time in Toryglen. They were both totally reliable and were great ambassadors in promoting the business amongst our hundreds of loyal customers in the district. We both owed them a huge debt of gratitude.

On Wednesday 28th October 1981, I had the happy experience of being reintroduced to the folk of St Andrew's, Motherwell for my Induction Service in the face of a large and expectant congregation. A most pleasing aspect of the evening was the presence of a good contingent of friends from both of my former congregations. The Penicuik group was headed by our dear friends, Douglas and Helen McRae, who had remained constant in our continuing friendship throughout the years since our departure from Penicuik. Another dear and good friend, Mary Hunt, whose friendship Rena and I treasured, was also representative of so many of my former members who elected to travel west and join us that night. From my congregation in Croftfoot, John Wallace, my former session clerk, accompanied by his wife Barbara, was present to speak movingly on my behalf. He was joined by a goodly number of my former office bearers and members. Margaret Williamson, my former clerk to the Congregational Board, accompanied by her husband Dennis, who had been an ever-supporting elder, were there that night, as were Pearl Smith, my former treasurer, and her husband Alec, another of the elders. I had created a youth club in my latter time at Croftfoot, and the Alstons, the McCullochs and the Mitchells, all part of one large family group who had been a driving force in assisting Rena and myself in this worthy cause, joined us on this very happy occasion. It was a real joy to have these former, fine office bearers and their wives present to share our happiness. The inauguration over, it was now down to work.

Before proceeding, it might be worth noting the terms and conditions, as it were, under which all ministry in the Church of Scotland is performed. The call I had newly received stated:

'We, the undersigned elders and members of the Church of Scotland congregation of St Andrew's,

Motherwell, by this call, which we willingly and heartily subscribe, invite you, Mr HUGH SAWERS, preacher and minister of the Gospel, to undertake the office of pastor among us; and we promise you all due respect, encouragement and obedience in the Lord, and that we shall use all the talents God has given us in Christian witness and Christian service for the maintenance of the Christian ministry and the furtherance of the Gospel.'

I would keep these high and holy aspirations before me as the new chapter opened.

In the wake of my previous experience, I was resolved to tread very warily in the midst of my new congregation that very evidently had neither the resources of mind nor of material goods that had so characterised my previous congregations. St Andrew's could be best described as a very ordinary, working-class community that drew its membership of approaching six hundred from throughout Motherwell. The defined parish comprised almost entirely local authority housing. One part of the parish was devoted to the Forgewood district of Motherwell that had been accurately described as one of the most deeply deprived areas of Europe. This was to be my sphere of pastoral oversight in the years that lay ahead. I had no false illusions as to the needs and demands that ministry in this environment would bring.

The church had escaped readjustment in the vacancy

simply by reason of the deprivation within which it was set and if it were to continue to be visible into an uncertain future, its general witness would need to be strengthened. I had confidence that, properly guided, my congregation would respond.

The Rev. John Cubie, who had, until days before, been my minister at Cambuslang Trinity, was to preach me in on the occasion of my first service at St Andrew's. He and I arrived at the church in good time and I led him into my new vestry which, in truth, was an appallingly decrepit little room set to the rear of our weary-looking church building. I knew John would be surprised and shaken when he laid eyes on my new sphere of operation. What was to follow though, more than caused him to raise his eyes. I pushed open the vestry door and disclosed to our sight a florid, heavily-built, elderly man seated at what was to be my desk. He did not raise his head in acknowledgement but continued studiedly to write on the pad before him. I met John's eye, and he was obviously totally bewildered by the continuing scene. After a short space, the seated figure raised his eyes, extended his hand whilst still remaining seated and said, with a note of intended authority towards John Cubie, 'Hello', and introduced himself. It was a most bizarre moment and I knew that I would very soon be involved in adjustments at St Andrew's. That event would have to wait. I had first to regain possession of my vestry. I bade 'Hello' in response, and then suggested that perhaps Mr Cubie and I could be left together to prepare for the service. The occupant, totally unabashed, happily gathered up his papers, stood up, and took his leave of us. I knew that I had moved into a quite different sphere of operation but how, I found myself asking, had the good folk of St Andrew's gone about the business of appointing senior office bearers?

One of my careful considerations before agreeing to apply for the charge was the fact that St Andrew's had always welcomed links with the Orange Order and a good number of their office bearers and members were committed to it. I had made it clear to the Vacancy Committee that I had no such affiliation or affection but I had no objection to the Orange Order attending the local church on the two or three occasions each year when they had traditionally paraded to St Andrew's. The committee had been satisfied by the assurance of willingness on my part to conduct these special services. The gentleman who was so at home in my vestry that first Sunday morning, I had to conclude, had come to think of himself as a sort of dilutee minister and had gradually embraced the trappings of the minister's vestry as part of his role. He did not prove difficult to readjust and, in that, he presented me with a very different encounter from that usually posed by men who had a view of their own worth and experience. In my further discussions with the gentleman, he presented a very respectful and wholly supportive attitude. He clearly regarded the Christian ministry very highly and it became quickly evident from our conversation that he bore no animosity whatever towards me. This may be measured when it became clear that I regarded his leadership as an interim measure and he was content to retire.

Early into my ministry the session clerkship became vacant, and there were two men of considerable capacity and spiritual maturity, already senior elders, who could be looked to in order that the Kirk Session be guided to a steady purpose. Mr Ian Darroch, who had a lifelong St Andrew's Church pedigree, was an accomplished speaker with a ready wit and he was possessed of high intelligence. On the debit side, Ian had a heart condition and the added responsibilities of the clerkship might not be appropriate. As I took soundings with him, he confirmed his reticence based on the health factor alone. He was looking to me in the good confidence that, working in all possible ways together, the congregation could be set on the right path.

Mr Jim Stewart had impressed me from my first encounter with him on the occasion of my induction. Jim Stewart had spoken but briefly that night but he spoke with clarity and conveyed the impression that he was an honourable, forthright and good Christian gentleman, and what better credentials, I had cause to reflect, would meet the needs of the office to which I would recommend through the Kirk Session, he accept. Happily for us at St Andrew's, Jim Stewart was prevailed upon to accept the office of session clerk.

I required to deal with the lassitude that pervaded the activities of the Kirk Session. Since a very relaxed and easygoing attitude permeated the fellowship, elders who had long since ceased to show any interest in the life of the church were still hailed as chums and fellow workers. 'Once an elder, always an elder' was the oft-played tune, and I reckoned it was time we struck a better note. I wrote to the entire eldership on 8th February, intimating a Kirk Session resolve that on Sunday 14th February there would be a collective act of eldership rededication in the face of the congregation. Opportunity was given for all who had detached for whatever reason to resurrect and renew their vows. Those who had difficulty should contact me so that we might discuss their position. In the interest of a lively and living fellowship, those who felt that they could not participate in the leadership, worship and service of the congregation should communicate to that effect and tender their resignation from the office of eldership.

There had been slackness and disorganisation within the Congregational Board when it came to the accounting associated with our freewill offering system and the open plate collections. I had partly been drawn to St Andrew's because not only were they in most elements impoverished socially but also they were impoverished financially, and the latter problem, I was certain, we could soon put right. I deemed it a privilege that Rena and I could support the congregation in sufficiently generous a fashion as to help alleviate their obvious hardship. We did this under the veil of secrecy that the weekly freewill offering system afforded. Such, however, was the impact of this new, unheard of level of giving that one of our office bearers bowed to temptation and helped himself to some easy pickings. He became so enthused, apparently, that he fell upon other envelopes that he discovered also contained sizeable sums. This, of course, was utterly reprehensible and immediate action was required. I obtained from the Weekly Freewill Offering Convener and from the congregational treasurer all the available evidence concerning the recurring incidents and we were distressed to discover the identity of the culprit. Both for his sake and the sake of his family, we did not want to expose his shame and so we devised a tightening up of our counting arrangements. Under the cover of the new procedure that required far fewer counters, we defined the new set-up as requiring people with particular skills in numeracy. Likewise, in the task of counting the ordinary open plate collection, only two assigned recorders were necessary. In this fashion, many of our folk were relieved of their involvement in the previous free-for-all. In consequence, the person responsible for our difficulty was dropped and nobody was ever made aware of our problem, save the small group who had highlighted our plight. Instantly, our offerings surged and, by the conclusion of 1982, our offerings were showing a massive and, in our church's terms, an historic rise of twenty-nine per cent. On the financial front, heads were being lifted and chests here and there were heaving with pride.

Chapter Thirteen

We marched forward in 1983, greatly encouraged on all fronts. I was finding preaching more satisfying than ever before and my congregation, as they scaled from the church on Sundays, were complimentary in a manner beyond any minister's proper expectations. Minister and people were in danger of creating a mutual admiration society. For my part, I valued their loyalty and their support.

Into the early summer we were looking to our holiday. Rena discovered from one of her pharmacy customers that her relative in America was aware that his local minister in Long Island was looking for an exchange during one of the summer months. We were put in contact and arranged to exchange pulpits and manses during July and into early August. I exchanged with the Rev. Louis Tuleja, a Congregationalist minister of Wading River, Long Island, who would preach in St Andrew's for the duration of my American visit. Douglas and Gillian joined Rena and myself for the trip. We were received by a most friendly and happy congregation who provided wonderful hospitality. The temperature each day touched 100°F and whilst the early-appointed hour for worship at 9.30 a.m. was welcome, the church was without air-conditioning and by the conclusion of the service I needed wringing out.

That discomfort apart, the whole experience was most memorable. For our last week we moved to Washington, where Louis Tuleja's daughter Lorraine was in the employment of the Republican Party machine at the Capitol. Lorraine and her friend, Gail, accommodated us in their flat and left us copious instructions, each concerning where we should be visiting. We did the major museums; visited the White House; visited both the Congress and the Senate whilst in session and, on our last day, experienced what comparatively few living Americans have ever done. We were granted a conducted tour up all the rickety inner ladders leading to the very pinnacle of the Capitol. Such trips are confined almost entirely to persons sponsored by, and accompanied also by, a senator or congressman. Lorraine had used her influence to attach us to Congressman Jerry Thomson from California who was treating his young son to the experience. As beneficiaries, we were afforded a spectacular all-round view of Washington.

Whilst we were having such a pleasurable time, my Motherwell people were truly magnificent in their reception of Louis and Ethel Tuleja who had returned to Wading River, just before we left, replete with stories of kindness extended and overwhelming hospitality. Jim and Margaret Stewart had been pre-eminent in their care of the Tulejas, and our next-door neighbours from our

Orchard Street manse, Dr John and Nettie Thomson, were also superb hosts and good friends as they have ever been towards us.

Beyond the pleasures of the summer, the most significant event at church was the ordination of twelve new elders on Sunday 4th December 1982. This event encapsulated the gain that was being achieved in the strengthening of our leadership. Of great moment was the fact that I ordained no fewer than nine ladies amongst the group. *The Motherwell Times* highlighted the family aspect of the Ordination Service, whereby either wife, daughter or son was joining no fewer than eight of our male elders in the Kirk Session. John Barr was being joined by his wife, Elma; Charles Brentnall by his son, William, and daughter, Betty; John Currie by his wife, Rita; Ian Darroch by his wife, Jean; Peter Hastie by his wife, Cathie and daughter, Karen; John Kerr by his wife, Ann; David Speirs by his daughter, Jean; and James Stewart by his son, Alistair. The ladies were the first ever lady elders in the previous male bastion of St Andrew's. The Spirit was moving in our midst and our people were glad.

Congregational offerings continued to move strongly with a gain at the year's end of fifteen and a half percent recorded. In the course of 1983, my past caught up with me and I was appointed Convener of Hamilton Presbytery's Stewardship and Finance Committee and, with this appointment, I returned as Presbytery representative to the Assembly's National Committee.

We at the manse celebrated two graduations in the course of the year. On Saturday 14th May, Rena graduated Bachelor of Arts from the Open University where she had applied herself to her studies with great effect. Gillian followed her mum to graduation when she was awarded her degree of Master of Arts from Glasgow University on Saturday 3rd December.

With our Kirk Session strengthened and reinvigorated, and in concert with the Congregational Board, it was decided that the tatty and crumbling vestry area to the rear of the church should be demolished and replaced by a new vestry complex comprising an attractive entry area, new vestry with toilet and storage accommodation, and a general purpose conference or choir room. This proposal represented tangible evidence of the growing confidence and self-belief in the congregation, and the idea was that, as far as humanly possible, this would be a self-help project. A former session clerk's widow, Mrs Annie Gillespie, was pleased for us to approach her architect son, Ian, who not only agreed to draw up the necessary plans but insisted in doing so without payment. The plans were swiftly forthcoming. Fund-raising was also speedily in place and, to push forward the venture, it was agreed that a vestry gift day would be held on Saturday 28th January 1984 from 10 a.m. until 1.00 p.m. when I would receive gifts in confidence from members willing to participate. I have indicated a little of the formerly impoverished nature of the congregation. In the event, I was busy throughout the allotted time span, receiving and recording gifts from innumerable and frequently elderly men and women who came forward with their gifts, sometimes small and often large, but in all cases with a sense of happiness and pride in their having a part to play in the new enterprise. To our amazement and gratification, my good people produced in excess of four thousand pounds that day, and they were, in turn, most happy to have a cup of tea or coffee and some home baking in appreciation for their generosity. The project was quickly underway and from start to finish it never lacked for both skilled and unskilled workers and labourers, and I was personally only too happy to labour with my fellow workers.

Lest it be thought that the folk of St Andrew's, by working mightily to put their own domestic house in order, were oblivious to the needs of others, let me assure you otherwise. I had guided the Congregational Board to prepare our congregation for participation in the General Assembly and Presbytery sponsored Christian Giving Plan. I, of necessity, had a place in the promotion of this plan by reason of my involvement as Presbytery Stewardship and Finance Convener and also by dint of my membership of the Assembly Committee. My own congregation followed my lead and in the months leading up the scheme's launch in April, teams of willing office bearers visited all the homes of our people and explained the plan and the needs it was designed to meet. The past two and a half years had witnessed a transformation in the financial strength of the congregation and the board had been able to make full provision for the claims on its resources in support of the Mission and Service Fund, and indeed went a little beyond the sum asked. This meant that a very good number of our loyal members had already increased their financial support as a consequence of information available to them explaining the wider work of the Church. They had already responded in advance of this new appeal being taken forward but crucially they, as ambassadors, were already committed and in a position to give a genuine lead. The outcome was dramatic and surpassed even their best hopes and expectations, with congregational offerings increasing by thirty-seven per cent by the end of December 1984.

Throughout the entire year of 1985, the vestry project took centre stage. I can do no better than recount Ian Darroch's report in our congregational newsletter. Ian was writing as the project co-ordinator:

'1985 will perhaps be remembered as the year we built the new vestry building at the rear of the church. However, the records show that we began the work of the project towards the end of 1984 and that the completion and dedication will take place in January 1986. During that time a great deal of work has been carried out by voluntary labour – demolitions, removals, drainage, excavations, foundations, concreting, building, etc., etc. – which involved much digging, shovelling, wheeling, lifting, mixing, carrying and general labouring. (All tasks to which muscles were, to say the least, unaccustomed.)

Members, adherents and friends of the congregation freely and unstintingly gave many of the various skilled crafts required, and such professional services as were necessary were procured as and when they were most economical.

Grateful thanks are due to all who have given their time and talents to further the progress, and to the ladies who, so often, have been there to provide delicious sustenance for the workers.'

I took immense pride in all the workers and helpers who had made such an obvious and enduring contribution to the enhancement of our church. Nor had they finished. When the building work was completed, lists of required furnishings and fittings were circulated amongst all our organisations and made available to individuals, should they desire, in order that they could provide a gift and, if appropriate, have it dedicated. Every specified item was freely provided. The net outcome was that I found myself in possession of a vestry such as I had not laid eyes upon elsewhere in my 'vestry' experience. It was a truly handsome room, beautifully equipped, with the centrepiece being a memorial desk and very superior chair, and sumptuously-carpeted floor. Given my previous aversion to involving my congregations in expense that, it could be thought I could benefit from, you might have expected me to resist this seeming extravagance. Not so in this instance. This outpouring of industry and goodwill I viewed as a wonderful therapy for my people. Since my arrival at St Andrew's, Rena, in the body of the church, was always impressed by the loving and all-embracing manner of how, when speaking of me, they always used the term, 'our minister'. To them I was never simply 'the minister'. It was their wish and purpose that 'their minister' should be properly housed at the church and to resist this desire would be have been totally ungracious. I placed on record my abiding appreciation of their thoughtfulness and generosity in this matter. We worshipped throughout the year in strong numbers and our elders' care and oversight pre-Communion had resulted in fine Communion attendances at quarterly celebrations of the sacrament.

I had been much engaged throughout the year on Presbytery business. I had been able to hone and refine my stewardship committee in the matter of oversight and encouragement to flagging congregations within Hamilton Presbytery. I, together with my very able partner, Mrs Nan Young, spearheaded our visitation groups, who reached out to situations needing help. The consequence was that we were soon witnessing a strengthening of support for the Mission and Service Fund within the bounds of Hamilton Presbytery.

Chapter Fourteen

The gloom of the long winter nights was well and truly lifted when, on Friday 31st January 1986, members and friends of the congregation assembled in very large numbers to witness the service of thanksgiving and dedication of our new vestry complex. The numbers involved were such that the meal provided for the occasion had to be planned for two sittings. As one half of the assembled congregation was entertained in church and then shown round the new premises, the other half dined. Then we reversed the process. All in all we had a memorable celebration of what had been achieved.

Our rarely noticed, erstwhile impecunious, congregation had raised £25,000 in little over a year and had built a building to the glory of God – a building that would have cost vastly more but for the input of so many of our good folk. As they carried forward this glow of achievement into 1986, the Congregational Board unveiled another project necessary for the ongoing good maintenance of our sanctuary. The church heating system was partial and quite ineffective. It was proposed that this should be replaced by an efficient electrical system and, yet again, experienced electricians were found within our fellowship who promptly offered their services. The work was undertaken over the summer and completed ahead of the severity of the incoming winter. The board provided materials, and all the labour was offered freely as an expression of personal stewardship by our talented electricians. I pushed ahead with Presbytery work and undertook a number of exhortative visits to congregations still mired through lack of funds.

At a National Church level, an issue involving a convicted bank embezzler and a convicted murderer had raised its head and I found myself troubled in the manner of its handling. Hamilton Presbytery had initially made national news by taking Mr Ian McDonald on trials for licence. Mr McDonald's case had been strongly supported by the Rev. John Harris, minister of St Mary's Church, Motherwell. John Harris was well placed as Mr McDonald's minister to know and understand all the background to Mr McDonald's conviction for embezzlement, but the main facts were well known, and Ian McDonald had not taken the bank's money to play 'Robin Hood' but had employed the proceeds of his crime for his own use. John Harris was the convener of the Presbytery's Church and Community Committee. This same committee was also giving strong support to the Assembly's Committee on Education for the Ministry in their advocacy that Mr James Nelson, who had been convicted of brutally killing his aged mother, should also be ordained as a minister of the Gospel. The arguments in favour of accepting both men into the Ministry of the

Church of Scotland were presented. It would be wrong and reactionary to fail to offer forgiveness in both cases. These men, it was allowed, had sinned; but both had repented and, upon all necessary scrutiny and assessment, it was judged that they would be worthy exemplars of the faith. Had not our Lord cautioned us on His approach to forgiveness; seventy times seven! We were to forgive without end. Furthermore, we could set a completely new example in terms of tolerance and insight.

The crowning argument and, from the advocate's point of view, it was intended to be unanswerable, was that we were being witnesses to the power of the Holy Spirit. The Holy Spirit, so the argument went, was moving powerfully and inexorably in our midst. My immediate thought concerning this powerful 'Holy Spirit' argument was that in all the tumult and distress occasioned by these difficult cases, the very strong likelihood was that the Holy Spirit would rest and would be in no hurry to promote the candidature of any further embezzlers and, for that matter, murderers. My thinking on this matter so far in the years since has been vindicated. The Rev. John Harris would doubtless be pleased to be designated a liberal within the parlance of Church politics. John, who in all my time at St Andrew's was an immediate near neighbour, occupying as we did manses in Orchard Street, was a highly gifted and a most accomplished speaker. He had the heightened capacity to present and follow through his argument with great clarity and it came as no surprise to his friends that he found himself a convincing figure in the National Church. His intelligence was not in question; I questioned his judgement on this most vexed matter. I was with him on the subject of Sin and Repentance and Forgiveness. I parted company with him on the issue of interpretation of the mind of the Holy Spirit. In all the circumstances and given the potential hammer blows to the sensitivities of our entire Church of Scotland fellowship, I judged that, as a redeemed embezzler and murderer caught up in the cleansing power of the Holy Spirit, total redress for all the sins involved could be given expression to in quiet Christian service. Had I been counselling Mr McDonald or Mr Nelson so early into their new-found spiritual liberation, I would have laid before them the price that their seeking ordination as a means of expressing their new commitment would necessarily impose upon the admittedly less-enlightened church communities throughout our land. If they could see their proposed action as creating a stone of stumbling to many, would they feel led to persist? Moral and ethical boundaries were being readjusted and frequently the churches could merely look on, helpless to intervene. Permissiveness had been driven forward relentlessly since the 1960s and was gripping the nation in vice-like fashion. These two men could provide a telling witness, not so much by leading but rather quietly and discreetly following in an ongoing act of atonement. On this issue the Church need not be helpless; it could be proactive in embracing the sinner but resolute in its guidance concerning the place of the redeemed, in the nature and the scope of the witness that was appropriate.

The Church, having due regard to procedures in place, decided in favour of the Education for the Ministry Committee's recommendation and Mr McDonald and Mr Nelson were duly ordained. I remain resolute that this decision did not assist forward the cause of our National Church but, to the contrary, caused dismay and unsettlement in the minds of untold thousands of our people. Another nail had been driven into the heart of the Church and not too many best positioned to do something about it appeared to notice.

Meantime, at St Andrew's, larger issues swept mainly over their heads and with continuing good humour those in office chided and encouraged the neglectful in their care. Care was an appropriate word because we operated a very active care committee under the immediate oversight of George and Cathie Anderson, both office bearers and stalwart workers for their church, and whose simple evangelical background suited them perfectly for their role in communicating the Master's love and favour upon those stricken or laid low. They and their team were constant and cheerful visitors to many a home in need of a loving visit. Mrs Rita Currie was another lady within our congregation who was ever on the lookout to head up some worthy cause within the church. Rita was an habitual fundraiser and presided with great effect over all our Christmas and summer fayres. Nobody was inclined to fail to respond to Rita's 'chivvying', which always had the stamp of good nature. With such folk in our midst it was little wonder that ours was a church without acrimony.

We saw the year through with the usual calls upon me for marriages and for funerals. There were many of the latter each year, not so many arising within our membership, but many more particularly from the Forgewood district, which, in terms of mortality, vindicated its miserable reputation for severe deprivation. There was infant mortality, which was ever distressing. Occasionally there was youth mortality, which sadly was sometimes self-induced through drugs or on occasion by suicide. Funerals against this background were difficult on account of the total detachment from the faith of the families involved. Understanding and comfort on the day was all they craved. Their lifestyle was so alien to the good order and reliance on the law which marked our ordinary church people. As the parish minister, the most I could hope to do was to visit them in their strickenness as the occasion demanded. Despite visitation to the homes in the district, we did not achieve any kind of harvest at all. If my congregation had depended for its survival on our parishioners in Forgewood, it would have long since died. Forgewood was our mission station and our missionaries were given a hard time.

At the end of the year, George Bell, our highly respected church treasurer for the last six and a half years, retired. George Bell was a superior kind of man in the very best sense. He had a fine appearance both in bearing and in dress; never less than immaculate. The outward appearance bore testimony to the inner man. Honour, truth and integrity, and care and consideration of others, were his hallmark. He was a man quietly and securely convinced of his faith who brought to his office a fine intelligence and grasp of his subject. We had been blessed and empowered by his work for us throughout his time in office.

George reported that our congregational income had moved forward in 1986 by eight percent and we continued to modestly exceed the sum invited for Mission and Service. As we advanced into 1987, I was much given to reflecting on how far I would be justified in pushing forward the witness of my people. I had, from the beginning of my ministry in their midst, been regarded as a kind of tornado sweeping away the flotsam of the past. From my point of view I had literally turned the throttle right down in recognition of how, ultimately, all progress comes at a cost.

As I drew upon the experience of driving forward my two previous congregations to the point when they wearied in their well-doing, I regarded it as imperative that I should not ruffle the feathers of my present congregation. Their good nature and happy collective disposition was their greatest asset. The church roll presented an interesting phenomenon and it was not unrelated to the situation, in this regard, I had found when I arrived in Penicuik. St Andrew's, being very much a family-orientated congregation, had a large number of 'dead' members still listed. The roll keeper jealously guarded the mysteries attaching to the make-up of the roll. Some still on the roll were, I discovered, literally dead. There appeared to be in the roll keeper's mind, a strange emotional reason why they had not been removed. Many others were dead in the sense that they could not apparently be raised to spiritual life and participation. What saved them from separation from our membership was their long nominal attachment and a strong family attachment to others in their wider family circle who were active and committed members. The latter had no desire to have their relatives, as they would see it, excommunicated. In my previous incarnation I would have dealt sympathetically but decisively in this matter. I proceeded with much greater caution in St Andrew's, and my office bearers, I detected, had no great heart for what, from restricted understanding, they would have looked upon as a witch hunt. I had to be reconciled to the fact that my failing to impress a strong and resolute lead on this issue would result in no measurable improvement in the chances of the congregation remaining viable into the future; the problem being that my folk were not much given to forward planning in this area. What mattered to them was how their church felt to them now, not how it might appear at some remote future date. I had, from the very beginning at Motherwell, decided that I would not push the frontiers too far but would rather proceed in what I hoped would be an effective, non-controversial, non-confrontational manner and assess in time the effectiveness or otherwise of this gentler approach. We had witnessed over the past years the fruits of this endeavour. My people were convinced that they had benefited, and I had most certainly benefited in the sense that I had been taken into their hearts and they had caused me no bother at all. The net effect of my adjusted approach was that my ministry had been totally comfortable and I was not at all stretched. If I had been looking toward a pleasant, uninterrupted idyll then I was experiencing just that. I had not, though, been called to an amenable and undisturbed life aimed in the direction of a distant retirement, having unsettled no one along the way.

I had to judge just how far forward I could lead my congregation without feeling that I was treading water. By the time 1987 arrived I was making an assessment along these lines. I wished to feel comfortable that I was worthy of my stipend and not merely the recipient of payment for a task that involved little effort or risk. After my peoples' Herculean fund-raising exploits, I discerned a slight easing on the oars, but I was anxious not to prejudice the comfort and satisfaction they clearly thought they deserved. Events took their natural course and I visited and ministered and preached and quietly led. Nobody was unhappy and congregational life exhibited its usual bustle and friendliness. On 16th May, I took particular pleasure in conducting the wedding of Netta Bryson, our church organist, to Bill Lithgow. Netta was our much-liked and highly regarded organist throughout my time in Motherwell. Organists and ministers can sometimes cross swords – witness my experience at

Croftfoot – but Netta was a mature young lady with a strong but kind personality, deeply committed to her faith, with whom it was a delight to share service. We, neither of us, had a contentious word throughout our working relationship and I was highly privileged to have the honour of conducting her marriage ceremony in her own church.

On the same theme, on Saturday 5th September in the chapel of Glasgow University, I was again privileged to conduct another wedding. On this occasion the bride was my future daughter-in-law, Karen Buttar, and the groom my son, Douglas. The families on both sides gathered, very hopeful indeed that the marriage of two young and mature adults who had known and loved each other from their early youth would be carried forward into the future attended by the blessing of God.

The year drew quietly and without incident to its close, and our income, it was noted, rose by a modest six percent. When 1988 dawned, I believed that, short of divine intervention, it would be my last year of ministry. I had long been convinced that my ministerial lifelong commitment to Christian stewardship, with all the avenues for expressing our faith that flow from it, was the singular contribution I could make to the Church. On our own domestic church front, I have already indicated the limitations I had felt constrained to impose on my leadership at St Andrew's. My people had done, and were doing, their very best, but I anticipated that I could not look to them for continual conspicuous support. I had, in effect, taken them as far as they could go, short of being driven, and I did not propose to drive them. I might be able to live with this lower key expectation if I could give continued free rein to my hopes for the Church at Assembly level where initiatives were sought and ultimately passed down to Presbyteries. I was, of course, a member of the Assembly Committee and from that vantage point could make a contribution to its thinking and its action.

The Assembly Stewardship and Finance Committee full-time secretary was the Rev. George Elliot who was immensely respected within the committee as a man of probity and utter integrity. George Elliot was a cultured gentleman of the old school who was ever thoughtful and considerate of those with whom he had dealings. He was ever polite and personable and I regarded him highly. We had never had a personal or intimate conversation so, apart from my work within the committee, ever in his presence, and the reputation which belonged to my obvious interest in stewardship, we were certainly not intimates. Then, just as Andrew Herron many years ago chose to arrange that we should share lunch together with, as I suspected, the intention being that he might, by this means better get to know me, so George Elliot at the conclusion of one of the Assembly Committees invited me to have lunch with him. I did not doubt but that George Elliot was interested in learning more about me and clarifying his mind concerning me. He might by this means secure a fair and accurate picture of the sort of man I really was, and George Elliot, fair-minded man that I took him to be, would for his own reasons wish satisfaction. Lunch, I am sure he thought, would be a help, but in the event there was to be no sharing since I had arranged, just an hour before his kind invitation, to have lunch with another committee friend. I judged that not even a potentially useful and important lunch with George Elliot, so unexpectedly offered, was sufficient reason to cancel my arrangement with a much lesser mortal. George Elliot's face registered disappointment when I indicated that unfortunately I was not free to accompany him. By declining, for whatever reason, I was not advancing my case for being in any way better understood. By the nature of their respective offices, George Elliot and the Assembly Convener were close working colleagues and, I suspect, good friends. In the months ahead I came to the conclusion that George Elliot, a man for whom I had the utmost respect and admiration, if pressed, would not have reciprocated in a similar fashion towards me. If this sensing of how, from limited acquaintanceship, he viewed me were correct, then I had to be disappointed indeed. I have, perhaps, laboured this point because it figured to a degree in my estimate that my usefulness to the Church, in the ways that I would have found productive, was to be limited. If this limitation could be justified for proper reasons then, of course, that would be entirely appropriate. If, however, the limitation or restriction on my leadership could be traced to personal animosity or any other such unworthy reason, then this would be altogether a different matter. All this speculation, I allow, is entirely subjective, but having assessed all available nuances and evidence, I was persuaded that further useful leadership involvement within the Assembly Committee would be hindered.

Chapter Fifteen

Meantime, 1988 had been reached and the office bearers and members of my congregation had no inkling of my evolving position that would soon result in my intimating my approaching retirement from the parish ministry. I was still being pulled in opposite directions. Could I justify to myself remaining at St Andrew's, like a machine just quietly ticking over? My overview of the predicament of the whole Church convinced me that the National Church was slowly and irredeemably lurching downhill. It seemed to lack both the vision and the determination to assail the forces ranged against it and I did not, in sounding this critical note, underestimate the insidious and persistent erosion in both public and private morality. The ethical dilemma confronting the Church was compounding with the passing of each year, and it was difficult to foresee an answer to this perplexity. On the other hand, if the captain has to be in place and go down with his ship then that captain should be an exemplar of all that is good and worthy within the tradition of his service. My experience of some of my colleagues who guided and controlled the affairs of our National Church persuaded me that the Church could, in the midst of all its difficulties, be better led. If I ask too much of our leadership then, alas, I remain unrepentant. The Christian ministry is not a career within which, as could be justified in commerce or industry, self-seeking is acceptable. The only acceptable aim within the faith is that we offer ourselves for service in the hope that God can make use of the talents with which He has endowed us. Experience has led me to believe that some senior colleagues in the Church, who could have influenced my future service, were persuaded that my views and approach were unacceptable to them for reasons to which I was not privy. What certainly was missing was a culture of frankness and openness. In accepting that I could be of no further use to the Church as represented by those who controlled the power structures, I simply had to resolve the issue of whether I could justify prolonging my ministry locally. My people in St Andrew's had been used under God to show the ninety or so congregations making up Hamilton Presbytery the latent possibilities for conspicuous service available to even so-called poor congregations. In the course of the past seven years our congregational income had tripled, and much wealthier congregations had looked on and acknowledged that if St Andrew's could achieve significant progress then should not they? Our corporate efforts had influenced, for the good, many other congregations within the bounds. Were I to remain at St Andrew's it would be alien to my nature for me to simply oversee a stagnating fellowship. I had perceptibly toned down the vigour of my leadership of my people after their quite splendid fund-raising exploits connected with their building project. I was open to the possibility that there would be a continued spillover over in terms of strengthened worship and giving, flowing spontaneously from that achievement. This did not happen. There was instead an almost measurable spiritual hangover. Our congregation had possibly travelled as far as was comfortable for them, and possibly one or two thought that a little slumber would not go wrong.

I finally decided that my input to the parish ministry had run its full course. Had I understood that I could have been used at a national level within the Church in promoting Christ's cause in the manner and with the directness and vigour I felt appropriate against the needs of the time, then I could have persuaded myself to remain with a good conscience at St Andrew's whilst fulfilling a parallel role for the wider Church. This latter route presented me with a 'no entry' sign and I did not feel called to be contentious or aggressive in pushing my prospectus.

I had emerged unscathed from the vicissitudes of my early life. I had been wondrously called into the Christian ministry. My years of service had provided me with access to men and women, my encounters with whom had added a tapestry of riches to my life's experience. Where else could I have secured the edifying closeness and friendship of those such as Dr William Steven and the Rev. James Munn? Where else could I have been so united in common cause with so many good and conspicuously honourable men and women in the worthy task of considering others? Twenty-five years had elapsed since my call and, paradoxically, as I had sought to serve, so was I served. What a wonderful faith! What a wonderful Saviour!

I intimated my approaching retirement to my Kirk Session in the first instance, and as befits such a loyal and supportive group, the question 'why' was not raised. I indicated that I had decided to retire early, and my session, in the midst of many expressions of regret and goodwill, wished nothing other than continued health and happiness to Rena and myself in that approaching retirement. We had been a good and happy and cohesive team throughout the years. Rena and I regarded our time spent at Motherwell the happiest and most fulfilling years we had spent together in Christ's service. My public ministry was about to end and we both shared the view that it had been profitable. I had been powerfully and inexorably called into the holy ministry and I was now being powerfully persuaded that, against the portents I recognised, now was the appropriate time to conclude. I gave due intimation of my decision to the Presbytery, indicating that I was desirous of retiring as from 31st July 1988. The usual procedures and courtesies were observed, and Hamilton Presbytery concurred with my request and agreed to the suggested retirement date.

Throughout the closing months of my ministry, I experienced a new freedom in addressing my people and alerting them to the challenges that lay ahead. I outlined a course of action based on continued fidelity in worship, service and giving that could provide a witness that the Presbytery could not ignore when coming to an assessment of the congregation's future.

On Sunday 3rd July 1988, I preached before my much-loved congregation for the last time. All such occasions are emotional, and this final one was no less so than any others that could be reported, save to say the evident good nature and open acceptance that so marked my arrival at St Andrew's was still happily in place as I took my leave of them.

The weeks and days before my retiral were marked most movingly for me by visits made to me by ordinary, sometimes little-known, members of the congregation who, apart from expressing gratitude for some remembered past service I had rendered, offered me, in the language of Motherwell, 'a minding'. Whilst on the subject of 'mindings', at the conclusion of my valedictory service and before we took our final leave of my folk over a cup of tea in the church hall, we were presented with characteristically generous gifts from the congregation. One such gift was a painting Rena and I had chosen to receive from the congregation. It was a watercolour by the well-regarded Scottish painter James Harrigan entitled *The Apple Pickers* and executed in Provence. Our church officer, Wesley Pollock, was invited by the person making the presentation to display it for the benefit of the congregation. Wesley dutifully brought forward the largish painting and looked completely perplexed. After a short space, he turned towards me and asked, 'Which way up?'

As I conclude, it would not be inappropriate to reflect on his question. I would have been honoured and delighted had my public ministry finished in a manner that could have elicited the response that of course is reserved singularly for Him of whom it was said, 'He turned the world upside down!' We labour in vain to emulate Him and never do. What a privilege, however, it is to enter the lists on His side and to identify with His cause as a minister of the Gospel.

My final word has to be a word of challenge addressed to us all. May your personal witness be such that by the time you are called to account for your stewardship you are able to say in concert with all the faithful, borrowing from the last words of our Lord on the cross, *Tetelesetai*, the Greek word and also the victor's word, meaning: *'It is finished!'*